"A quick, joyful, and inspiring read! Peppered with student art examples, Leslie shares how school counselors can use art therapy approaches to increase equity, access, and create joy for each and every student, no previous art experience required. Leslie builds the foundation of how and why art therapy is beneficial to students and adults and shares practical guidance on how to use art therapy approaches within the confines of busy school schedules, tight funding, and limited space. A great resource for those who already use art in their practice and for those brand new to it. A must-add to your school counseling library!"

Gretchen Rhodes, *Director of School Counseling,*
Chicago Public Schools

"In this book, Leslie shares her joy in using art therapy strategies to help students thrive. This is a must-read for school counselors looking to grow their skills, and use art to reach their students in new and meaningful ways. Leslie makes it easy to see how art can bring new dimension to the theories and standards our profession is built on. I came away ready to implement her art activities with my own students, and feeling inspired – I know readers will feel that too."

Lisa Delgadillo, *School Counselor, Licensed Clinical Professional*
Counselor, ASCA 2025 School Counselor of the Year Finalist

I0130466

Integrating Art Therapy Approaches in School Counseling

Using this book, school counselors can increase their knowledge on the benefits of art therapy approaches in school counseling. This book serves as a frame of reference for school counselors to use throughout their careers, as it includes examples of integrating art into direct school counseling services, art directives and prompts, case studies, and how to process art in a safe and inclusive way within the school counselor role.

While gaining an understanding of the history of art therapy, readers will learn how the use of art in school counseling practice aligns with the American School Counselor Association (ASCA) National Model to support student achievement and overall well-being. The author holds a master's degree in art therapy and licensure in school counseling and speaks on behalf of both fields and their benefits, allowing for school counselors to incorporate art therapy-informed practices into their program.

Readers will recognize that art is a valuable resource to obtain the information they need from students in a creative way, and as an alternative and/or supplement to the traditional talk therapy counseling session.

Leslie de Vera Arroyo, MAAT, LCPC, is a school counseling specialist for the Chicago Public School District in Illinois, USA.

Integrating Art Therapy Approaches in School Counseling

Leslie de Vera Arroyo

Routledge
Taylor & Francis Group

NEW YORK AND LONDON

Designed cover image: Getty Images

First published 2026
by Routledge
605 Third Avenue, New York, NY 10158

and by Routledge
4 Park Square, Milton Park, Abingdon, Oxon, OX14 4RN

Routledge is an imprint of the Taylor & Francis Group, an informa business

© 2026 Leslie de Vera Arroyo

The right of Leslie de Vera Arroyo to be identified as author of this work
has been asserted in accordance with sections 77 and 78 of the Copyright,
Designs and Patents Act 1988.

All rights reserved. The purchase of this copyright material confers the right
on the purchasing institution to photocopy pages which bear the photocopy
icon and copyright line at the bottom of the page. No other parts of this book
may be reprinted or reproduced or utilised in any form or by any electronic,
mechanical, or other means, now known or hereafter invented, including
photocopying and recording, or in any information storage or retrieval system,
without permission in writing from the publishers.

Trademark notice: Product or corporate names may be trademarks or
registered trademarks, and are used only for identification and explanation
without intent to infringe.

ISBN: 978-1-032-55492-1 (hbk)
ISBN: 978-1-032-55491-4 (pbk)
ISBN: 978-1-003-43094-0 (ebk)

DOI: 10.4324/9781003430940

Typeset in Times New Roman
by codeMantra

To my son Adé and all the youth, you are the future.
May you express yourselves creatively.

Contents

Acknowledgments

I remember years ago I wrote on a post-it note that I was going to write a book about art therapy in school counseling and stuck it on my corkboard. Thank you, God, for answering and providing a path for me to accomplish this.

Of course, it didn't come easily and I could not have done this work on my own. Soraida, my bestie, thank you for allowing me to vent about how hard this whole process was for me. Sitting at cafes on weekdays after a long day of work and on weekends helped me to stay motivated and focused. The frequent breaks to catch up on life and accompanying laughs helped tremendously.

Thank you to my son's father, Adrian, who was a huge support when I went back to school to obtain my licensure as a school counselor. Your sacrifice allowed me to jump-start a career I had no idea I could be so passionate about. Also, thanks for helping me get the photos for this book print-ready.

Thank you to my writing coach and developmental editor, Heather Marie Evans, for helping me find my voice and encouraging me to come front and center instead of "hiding behind others' words." These were lessons for writing and life. Thank you to Amanda Savage, Editor, for seeking me out at the American School Counseling Association Conference and believing that I had something to share in the form of a book.

I'd like to thank the following from Chicago Public Schools: Gretchen Rhodes, Liliana Ponce, and Dr. Heidi Truax, from the Office of School Counseling and Postsecondary Advising, for helping me share my knowledge of art therapy with school counselors across the district. Gretchen – additional thanks for reading the manuscript and providing valuable feedback. Thank you to all of the school counselors who were part of the pilot and research programs, whose names I will not share to protect the privacy of their students. Your ability and willingness to embrace student art into your practice have been remarkable. Thank you to Aribania Cosey and Lisa Delgadillo, school counselors, for reviewing my book proposal, and Lisa for taking the time to read the entire manuscript and for your support. Thank you to Frederick Williams, my former principal. Because of your leadership and understanding of the school counselor role, I was able to be the school counselor I always wanted to be and maximize my art therapy background to address student needs.

Finally, my immediate family: My son, Adé, who put up with me for two and a half years as I jokingly, but not so jokingly, asked him to write this book for me. He graciously declined every time and reminded me that I was the only one who could do it. Thank you, Adé, for being you. I am so proud of you and that keeps me motivated. Thanks to my brother Michael for gifting me what I call my "Mighty Mac" equipment, which allowed me to input all my thoughts and ideas, as chaotic as they came at me. Also, having the custom keyboard that you taught my son to put together made typing away enjoyable. To my parents, immigrants from the Philippines, for insisting on coming to the United States, facing all the challenges that came with adjusting to a new country, and doing the best they could to make sure that my brother and I had access to opportunities that we wouldn't have had otherwise. Thank you so much.

Introduction

You're walking down the hall and you see a student sitting on the ground against the wall. They appear sullen, head down, shoulders slumped, and staring at the ground. A well-intentioned staff member asks, "What's wrong with you today?" The student remains silent and shrugs their shoulders. The staff member responds, "Well, I can't help you if you don't tell me what's wrong."

Unbeknownst to the staff member, this is a case more complicated than a student simply refusing to answer. It can be difficult to verbally access what is distressing at any moment in time, if not impossible. The school setting is a place where many can feel they do not belong, making expressing feelings scary, daunting, and incredibly vulnerable. We ask students how they are feeling all the time, but often do not give them a different way to communicate their emotions to us.

It has been my mission to demonstrate how integrating art therapy approaches into school counseling practice can help students, school counselors, and our school ecosystems at large. It opens a door for students to express their feelings in a non-verbal way and helps school counselors gain access to their students' deepest thoughts, enabling them to support their students creatively, effectively, and efficiently across American School Counseling Association (ASCA) Ethical and Student Standards.

As a school counselor, you may have already started using art in your practice as a way for students to communicate and demonstrate their thoughts, feelings, ideas, knowledge, interests, and hopes for the future. If so, you've most likely witnessed the increase in focus and sense of calm that your students demonstrate as they create art. You may have also used student art as a way to form connections, whether with you as the school counselor or amongst the students. Overall, the benefits of art when working with students are nothing new to you. Picking up this book may be a way for you to deepen your understanding of art therapy, a field that is research-based and has been shown to positively impact the mental health among diverse populations for decades (Hu et al., 2021; Shukla et al., 2022; Uttley et al., 2015). Though this book does not prepare you to become an art therapist, as that would require a specialized degree, it can provide guidance on how to use art intentionally with students in a safe and effective way aligned

DOI: 10.4324/9781003430940-1

to your role as a school counselor. It will serve as a resource on how to use student art and integrate art therapy-based techniques to maximize the impact of school counseling services.

Or, perhaps you have never used art as a school counselor and have reservations about introducing the medium into your practice. You are unfamiliar with art directives and prompts, and you are unsure how to set up an art-making space. You question what art materials to use and how. After all, you have not received formal education in visual arts. You may ground your practice in different therapeutic modalities, such as person-centered therapy or cognitive behavioral therapy, yet you are uncertain on how to align art therapy with your approach.

It may be reassuring to know that the value of art therapy does not rely on technical artistic skill. Art therapists do have an educational background in the visual arts, making them knowledgeable of the wide range of art media, materials, and supplies that help to inform treatment for their clients. However, art therapy approaches described in this text will largely cover art materials that many school counselors have used with students, such as markers, colored pencils, paint, with perhaps one or two new art mediums introduced in this book. Additionally, the value in integrating art into counseling practice does not lie in creating an aesthetically pleasing piece of work. There is no right or wrong, and the created artwork is used for insight for both the student and the counselor, providing information that is not typically accessed through verbal or written means. In this case, this book will provide ideas and resources to ease the incorporation of art into practice in hopes that you will gain confidence in the ability to integrate art therapy-informed strategies.

The aim of this book is to inspire the integration of art therapy approaches in school counseling practice as a simple, effective, and transformative way to meet the ever-evolving needs of students. In recent years, school counselors have reported an increase in challenges to meet the academic, social/emotional, and career needs of students. With the lingering effects of the global pandemic, recent light on systemic racism, teacher and other staff shortages, and the current political climate, school communities experience the impact on students and staff alike (Akgul et al., 2021) (U.S. Department of Education & Cardona, 2021). School counselors find themselves with an increased number of student referrals for behavioral health, attendance, and other issues impacting academic achievement. As such, school counselors can benefit from increasing their knowledge of creative interventions and strategies to meet the demands of their role in a way that benefits all students.

1.1 Who Am I? The Art of Bridging Art Therapy with School Counseling

It has been quite a windy road to get to where I am, though everything seemed to come full circle. Before becoming a School Counseling Specialist for the

Chicago Public School District, my career began when I graduated with a Master of Arts in Art Therapy from the University of Illinois in 1999. This program was the first of its kind in Chicago, founded by Harriet Wadeson, Honorary Life Member (HLM) of the American Art Therapy Association (AATA). I remember the initial shock when I received a phone call from Harriet herself, informing me that I was accepted into the program. Being born on the south side of Chicago, I wanted to practice art therapy in a city so diverse, rich in culture and history, and a place where I could see art therapy being beneficial in one of the largest cities in the country.

In the years before being accepted, as an undergraduate, I was pursuing a pre-medicine track with a major in biology. I soon realized that it wasn't going to work out, as I found myself drawing the diagrams and photos from my biology textbook rather than reading the contents in it. I have always loved drawing, ever since I was little. I loved to observe people, places, and things, and create my experiences of them on paper. Anything I found interesting or fascinating to look at, whether a beautiful dress or a church building, I found solace in the process of drawing the subject in my sketchbook. But it was ingrained in me growing up from my well-meaning parents that art was just a hobby. To them, job security and financial prospects as an artist were considered slim to none compared to one in the healthcare field.

I knew I wanted to be in some type of helping profession, and what I learned through my psychology class was that being in the medical field wasn't the only way to achieve this. I loved studying for my psychology class, much in a way I thought I'd be for my other science classes. I was fascinated by how thoughts and feelings affect human behavior, and by understanding this, we can help others understand themselves more, increase their confidence and self-awareness, improve their relationships with others, and improve their mental health. I started to wonder if art and psychology could be combined in some way. The two together made sense to me, as creating art was my place of peace, and I wondered if that could somehow be part of an actual job helping people feel better about themselves. I don't recall the moment I discovered art therapy was a career. It may have come up in my research of careers to pursue with a psychology or art degree. Once I made this discovery, there was no more research to be done. I immediately changed my major to psychology with a minor in art to prepare for a graduate program in art therapy.

Although I was passionate about sharing the therapeutic benefits of art therapy with the world, my graduation bubble burst when I realized how difficult it was to find a job with the title of an "art therapist." At that time, people were still not seeing the value in art therapy in different settings. However, I ended up working at a hospital where I completed my art therapy internship as an "activity therapist" for the inpatient and psychiatric units of the hospital. I soon found out that my unpaid art therapy internship was different from my employment, as the head of the department was not keen on having too much art as an "activity," favoring exercise, board games, and well, pretty much anything other than art. These activities were not of less importance, but I didn't believe that I was maximizing my education, expertise, and experience.

Fortunately, since the art therapy program was set up so that I could sit for licensure in counseling, my next position was a substance abuse counselor. At the time, I wanted to integrate art therapy into existing groups at the center, though the director advised that I didn't bring in paint as that would ruin the floors. At that point, I felt discouraged in using any of my art therapy background at all and focused my energy on obtaining my licensure in counseling, as that seemed to gain more attention when seeking a job in the mental health field.

After three years I felt burnt out and discouraged, and left the substance abuse center on my own accord. I took a trip to Spain, despite my bank account's advice, to find myself, my purpose, and improve my Spanish-speaking skills. I remember studying Spanish in Málaga, the hometown of Picasso, which seems fitting when I think of it now. I often include Picasso's quote, "Art washes away from the soul the dust of everyday life," in workshops and conference presentations to highlight the healing and cathartic aspect of making art. I was lost, and I believe my soul was very dusty during my time in Spain. You could even see it in the watercolor paintings I attempted of the beaches of Málaga; the brushstrokes appeared light, constrained, and reserved.

As funds dwindled, I returned to the States. I became a clinical therapist working with families brought together by adoption, where I was able to integrate more art therapy into the role. Through the art created by these families, I was able to see their family dynamics as well as the grief and loss experienced by the adopted children over their biological parents. However, during this time I recognized that the children I worked with were struggling academically and/or behaviorally, and that no one at their schools knew what they were going through in their personal lives.

This is when I began to think about how I could do my work in schools. After all, I remember the numerous adults I met when working in the hospital and in the substance abuse center sharing how they first experienced abuse, neglect, or some type of trauma early in life. Seeing as schools can be the first place where students can learn to make positive choices that will impact their futures, as well as the place where youth display that something could be wrong, I knew that I wanted to take my work to the school setting.

I went back to school to train as a school counselor. Shortly after receiving licensure, I started as a school counselor in an elementary school. I was able to integrate my art therapy background with small groups and individual counseling, supporting students early in any challenges impacting their progress in school. However, as budgets tightened, I was assigned more duties in my role, many of which were considered inappropriate duties for school counselors. They did not require an educational background or experience in school counseling, and as a result, students had limited access to counseling services. Nonetheless, these duties, such as case management, test coordination, and record keeping, were prioritized over providing counseling services such as classroom instruction and small groups for students. So not only did I get farther away from the intentional use of art therapy, I also got farther away from intentional, proactive school counseling. Even when I switched from an elementary to a high school setting, thinking I'd be able to provide more counseling, I found that the overall view of the school counselor role was the same. The counseling that I did provide was reactive, addressing crisis situations as they arose. It became overwhelming as the only staff member in the building to have the training to address these crises on a given day. Yet, this is where I saw the true power of art therapy approaches in school counseling. When students were going through distress, I was able to gain insight into their needs through their art in a shorter period of time than I would have if I only used traditional talk therapy methods.

Fortunately, after years of advocacy by school counselors and leaders in the district, the role has slowly become recognized and duties started to align with the American School Counselor Association National Model. My last school was where I was able to best utilize my art therapy background in school counseling. I had a supportive principal who understood the role, appreciated my background in art therapy, and even provided the classroom where the art classes were previously held as my entire office. I was lucky to have an abundance of art supplies left from the previous art teacher, and I was set up to do my work and combine my two career loves: art therapy and school counseling.

Now, I am a School Counseling Specialist for the Chicago Public School District. I took this role after 14 years of serving as a school counselor in both elementary and high school settings, and right at the height of the pandemic. In this role, I've had the privilege to advocate for the school counseling field among district leaders, emphasizing the importance of student access to school counseling services in every school building in the district. I've been involved in the development of district-wide training to align school counseling programs to the ASCA Model, credentialing on equitable post-secondary advising, best practices such as how to respond to local and national crises as a school counselor. I've been part of teams that developed district-wide initiatives regarding mental health and schools as healing spaces. The most rewarding part of my job though, has been the opportunity to train school counselors on the foundations of art therapy and how to safely and appropriately take what art therapists have always known about art, and integrate it in their practice within the scope of their role.

1.2   Birth of a Book

When I was approached at a conference to write a book, it was hard to believe at first. After all, I started my career in positions that didn't seem to want to hear about art therapy at all. In comparison, I am now presenting on integrating art therapy and school counseling to rooms at full capacity, filled with colleagues who are intrigued, interested, and excited to hear about the positive impacts. Perhaps the times have finally brought forth the importance of well-being and mental health in all aspects of life. With school counseling books coming to the forefront that emphasize the importance of trauma-informed practices, or how to work through systemic racism, we are growing to recognize that successful school counseling comes from treating our students as whole, complex, and multi-faceted people who have more than one way to communicate, express, and demonstrate their emotions and knowledge.

So, I wrote this book to add to this growing but increasingly important literature. I am not writing to say that art therapy approaches will solve everything in our field. However, I believe integrating art therapy approaches into counseling practices is a step in the right direction to support all our youth. This is a contribution to education, albeit small, to demonstrate that by being open to all the different possibilities of learning, we can embrace creativity, flexibility, and spontaneity that will help our youth to achieve their full potential, be resilient in life's challenges, and become positive contributors to society.

1.3   What This Book Is...and Isn't

Before diving into how to use this book, it's worth mentioning first what this book is and what it is not. The "art" in art therapy within the context of this book pertains to visual art, and is not to be confused with Expressive Arts Therapies or Creative Arts Therapies. The latter is inclusive of various forms of art – dance, drama, music, and the visual arts. This book will provide an overview of how art therapy and how visual pieces of art are created as part of the therapeutic process. This is meant to be more intentional about using art in school counseling practice based on the research and practice that the art therapy field has contributed for years.

What this book is not is a recipe book filled with lessons. You will see some lessons referred to in the Appendix, but it is not a book with magic lessons that resolve any issue at hand. Students, like all humans, are complex. Many of the art directives I've used were sparked in my mind as I learned more about the students and what they needed. As a school counselor, you need to remain creative and responsive to your students. That's the remarkable thing about art and creativity, with its ability to adapt at any moment to the unique needs of each person. Our students' needs and the way they learn and thrive are evolving on a daily basis. Because of this, the reliance on a set activity, lesson, or curriculum to address the matter at hand can be futile. Trusting our instincts as professionals, and deepening our understanding of students is what makes our work impactful. We have to accept that we may need to pivot unexpectedly from what we originally planned, whether in the classroom or working with the students in a small group or individual counseling. By doing this, we open the door to realizing a student's full potential, mostly for themselves, as the student's art helps them see their strengths, and in turn helping them see the opportunities and possibilities for their futures.

I.4   How to Use This Book

Although you may want to skip to chapters that include art directives and practical advice on processing art, I strongly encourage you to read the chapters in chronological order. Each chapter builds on from the next, and you will gain the most from this book by going through the whole journey front to back.

Part I is where you will learn the foundations of the art therapy field, including theory, practice, and research. This key context will help you understand the "why" behind the art directives in the later chapters, and it will also help you fully embrace the meaning of using art with your students. It will allow you to recognize the importance of being flexible in your approach, shifting your practice when you begin to gain more insight to your students and what they need.

Chapter 1 outlines the history and development of the art therapy field, demonstrating how this evidence-based approach has had positive impact on mental health for many years.. This is reviewed to increase your awareness of the scope of art therapy as well as showing how school counseling and art therapy align with one another. Chapter 2 will focus on how art therapy approaches help school counselors meet the ASCA Ethical Standards. This chapter demonstrates how using art can help school counselors meet these standards when it comes to equitable and culturally responsive practices, catering to the unique needs of diverse school populations. As neuroscience in recent years has backed the validity of art and its impact on well-being, in particular for those who have experienced trauma, a discussion of integrating art therapy as a trauma-informed practice through an equitable lens will also be discussed.

Chapter 3 will focus on how art therapy approaches can help students learn the ASCA Student Standards. This is referred to as the core competencies, otherwise known as the 36 Mindsets and Behaviors that contribute to students' college and career success. Integrating art therapy-based interventions can help students develop these mindsets and behaviors as they relate to three main domains: academic, social/emotional, and career. This chapter demonstrates how art therapy approaches can be applied throughout the tiered levels of school counseling service: Tier I, universal programming that reaches all students, such as classroom instruction, and Tier II Services, such as small group and individual counseling. Case studies demonstrate how art therapy approaches can be easily integrated into school counseling services to address student standards.

Part II is dedicated to what art therapy approaches integrated with school counseling look like in practice. Chapter 4 will begin with setting up a safe and trusting environment to embrace the student and their art, before any art directives are discussed. Having students complete art by a school counselor who establishes this environment first and foremost will enhance the art-making process and maximize the benefits as a whole. This is contrary to simply inserting art as part of a lesson, or following pre-set lessons and art a la carte. After a safe and trusting environment is established, factors within the physical environment will be addressed, including space considerations and art materials.

From there, Chapter 5 will discuss the "art" of processing art. We will explore how art serves as an extension of the student, showcasing their internal world. The art can be used to form connections with others in a safe and less frightening way than having to rely only on verbal or written communication. This chapter will explore how school counselors can utilize students' artwork to process and gain deeper insights into their identities, emotions, and experiences. It will also provide guidance on how counselors can assist students in interpreting their art themselves, increasing their self-awareness and self-identity. After exploring the ethical considerations of processing students' art, examples of questions and prompts that allow students to feel safe and comfortable sharing the significance of their artwork will be discussed. The reader will learn non-judgmental approaches to the student's artwork and how to use different counseling theories to guide their practice, such as using cognitive behavioral, person-centered, and solution-focused brief therapy theories, in all settings: working in a classroom, small groups, and individual counseling sessions. It concludes that the successful processing of the art within school counseling services will allow students the autonomy to express and communicate their needs, leading the school counselor and student to recognize ways to meet them.

Finally, Chapter 6 will provide a window to the possibilities of embracing art into school counseling practice. School counselors maintain skills through professional development to stay informed on research and evidence-based practices to meet students' evolving needs. Learning art therapy approaches through training allows the school counselor to experience the benefits firsthand. When given the time to process their art with a colleague, it also provides for self-awareness and self-care. The work of a school counselor can be overwhelming and exhausting, which is a major factor contributing to the school counselor shortage nationwide. This chapter will showcase school counselors' participation in training where they participate in the art-making process, increasing their knowledge of the benefits and how to use art intentionally to enhance their practice, feeling more equipped to do the work at hand.

1.5 A Note on Anonymity

To protect confidentiality, case studies presented in this book will be a combination of the author's experiences and those of school counselors' experiences who participated in a pilot study integrating art therapy approaches in their practice. Artwork presented in this book is either a mock-up of cases often seen in my own experiences and of students who participated in the pilot study and whose consent was provided by parent or guardian, and students themselves (ages 13 to 17 y.o.). Pseudonyms were assigned to these case studies to further protect the identity of students.

1.6   A Note on Supervision

Though this book is written to enhance your already existing counseling skills, when attempting to integrate anything new, make sure to seek out supervision for professional feedback as you implement art therapy approaches.

1.7   Pause and Reflect

Before you go on to Chapter 1, I'd like to encourage you to pause and reflect on a time, if any, when you had a student or group of students create art while providing counseling services.

1   Do you remember why you used art-making as part of your counseling session or classroom instruction?
2   Did you notice anything different about your student as they engaged in the art-making process? Did you notice the students' ability to follow the art directive given?
3   Were they focused?
4   Did they appear calm?
5   Were they more or less talkative in the process?
6   Did your student feel confident about their work of art?
7   Were they excited to talk to you about the art?
8   Or did they express disappointment in their art?

As you read through the next chapters, I hope that you'll gain deeper insight into the responses to the above questions and ultimately be inspired to use art therapy approaches in school counseling.

References

Akgul, T., Brown, J., & Karch, L. (2021). The personal and professional impact of COVID-19 on school counselors: An exploratory study. *The Interactive Journal of Global Leadership and Learning*, 2(1), 1–31. https://doi.org/10.55354/2692-3394.1024

Hu, J., Zhang, J., Hu, L., Yu, H., & Xu, J. (2021). Art therapy: A Complementary treatment for Mental Disorders. *Frontiers in Psychology*, 12, 1–9. https://doi.org/10.3389/fpsyg.2021.686005

Shukla, A., Choudhari, S. G., Gaidhane, A. M., & Syed, Z. Q. (2022). Role of art therapy in the Promotion of Mental Health: A Critical review. *Cureus*, 14(8), e28026. https://doi.org/10.7759/cureus.28026

U.S. Department of Education, & Cardona, M. A. (2021). *Supporting child and student social, emotional, behavioral, and mental health needs*. U.S. Department of Education. https://www2.ed.gov/documents/students/supporting-child-student-social-emotional-behavioral-mental-health.pdf

Uttley, L., Scope, A., Stevenson, M., Rawdin, A., Buck, E. T., Sutton, A., Stevens, J., Kaltenthaler, E., Dent-Brown, K., & Wood, C. (2015). Systematic review and economic modelling of the clinical effectiveness and cost-effectiveness of art therapy among people with non-psychotic mental health disorders. *Health Technology Assessment, 19*(18), 1–120. https://doi.org/10.3310/hta19180

Part I

Foundations of Art Therapy and School Counseling Theory and Practice

Chapter 1

Foundations of Art Therapy

Why is it important to know the origins of art therapy? Of course, you could incorporate one or two art activities into existing individual or group counseling sessions, or even into classroom lessons to add variety to students' learning experiences. However, interweaving these activities into your sessions with the understanding of the field's development, research, and leading voices will provide an opportunity to truly embrace the benefits of art therapy on growth, well-being, and mental health for students. Drawing from my experience in both art therapy and school counseling, I'm eager to share insights that can support school counselors who are already using art as part of their practice, and all those interested in exploring its therapeutic potential. Understanding the origins of art therapy can provide increased awareness of the effectiveness of integrating it to help students navigate their PreKindergarten to 12th-grade journey and set them up to be successful in school and in life.

In this chapter, we will explore what art therapy is, its origins, how art is therapeutic for different age groups, and how art therapy can be beneficial when used in an educational setting. We will also address some common misconceptions about art therapy to remove any barriers to learning its potential when integrating approaches in school counseling. Once again, it's important to note that you will not become an art therapist as a result of reading this book, as that would require an advanced specialized degree in art therapy, including hours of supervision in practicing art therapy. Rather, the goal is to better understand how art therapy approaches can be integrated into your school counseling practices, appropriate to your role, to benefit all students regardless of age, race, cultural background, or learning abilities. Finally, you can explain the rationale behind integrating art therapy to key team members, such as administration, teachers, students, other school staff, and parents. Providing education on how art therapy approaches enhance student success will strengthen support and collaboration in your role as a school counselor.

DOI: 10.4324/9781003430940-3

1.1 What Is Art Therapy?

To put it simply, art therapy is the combination of art and psychology. Accordingly, an art therapist is trained in both art and psychological theory, with the addition of facilitating the creative process as a means of expression and communication. According to the American Art Therapy Association (AATA), the field of art therapy helps to improve the mental health of individuals, families, and communities of all ages, including children and adults, through the creative process of art-making, the application of psychological theory, and built upon a psychotherapeutic relationship between the client and the art therapist (About the American Art Therapy Association, 2023). Since the birth of the field, art therapy has been researched and found to be effective in times of distress, to alleviate symptoms of depression and anxiety, and to increase mental focus among diverse populations (About the American Art Therapy Association, 2023). As a result, art therapy is practiced in various settings, including hospitals, nursing homes, outpatient treatment centers, and schools. So, how did it all begin?

1.2 Origins of Art Therapy

The first person to use the term "Art Therapy" was Adrian Hill, a British artist and war veteran, when he discovered the therapeutic quality of art-making while recovering from tuberculosis in a sanatorium in 1938 (Bitonte & Santo, 2014). He found painting as an outlet due to its healing quality and encouraged other patients recovering from tuberculosis to create art for themselves. He wrote about these experiences in 1945 in "Art versus Illness: A Story of Art Therapy," where he described how the patients grew to appreciate art, whether or not they considered themselves as having artistic abilities (Adrian Hill, UK Founder of Art Therapy by Morgan Bush, Intern, n.d.). He was employed as the first official art therapist in 1946 by the Netherene, a state psychiatric hospital in the United Kingdom. He later became the president of the British Association of Art Therapists.

In the U.S., Margaret Naumberg used the term around the same time as Hill. Naumberg's early work started at the Walden School, which she established in New York and focused on developing children's capacities rather than their ability to retain knowledge (Margaret Naumburg, n.d.). She built her ideas of art therapy on the theories of psychotherapy originating from founding fathers, Sigmund Freud and Carl Jung (Junge & Asawa, 1994, as cited in Vick, 2003). She considered the resulting art product as "symbolic speech," or a client's unconscious thoughts, ideas, and feelings brought to conscious awareness (Junge, 2016). Naumberg is widely known among art therapists as the "Mother of Art Therapy" for defining art therapy as "art psychotherapy." Art brought to the surface underlying and repressed experiences, thoughts, and emotions that were causing the client distress daily. Through its visible and tangible form,

Naumberg emphasized the therapeutic benefits of using art as a reference to the unconscious, open for interpretation and analysis between the client and art therapist (Naumberg 1950/1973 as cited in Vick, 2003).

Edith Kramer, another key figure in the art therapy field, also had roots in psychotherapy, drawing on the work of Freud and Jung. However, her approach was different in that Naumberg considered the therapeutic benefits of art therapy to come from the process itself rather than the completed art piece. Kramer was a painter who fled from Hitler's Germany in 1938 to Prague, where she began to teach art classes to refugee children (Junge, 2016). It was there she recognized the healing quality of making art. She described this as the "art as therapy" approach, emphasizing the therapeutic aspect comes through the creative process of making art and the completed art as a by-product.

1.3   Art in Education

Much of the beginning of art therapy was psychoanalytically based, but once psychoanalytic writers emphasized the impact of early childhood experiences on human development, personality, and behaviors, art therapy naturally made its way to the educational field (Junge & Asawa, 1994 as cited in Vick, 2003). The scientific study of childhood began in the late nineteenth century when the idea emerged that education should consider "the whole child." Called "Progressive Education" (Dewey, 1958 as cited in Junge, 2016), this philosophy advocated for learning through doing. New teaching methods were developed based on respect for the child's creativity and included an emphasis on the arts (Junge, 2016) along with the overall development of children (Cane, 1951/1983; Lowenfeld, 1987 as cited in Vick, 2003).

Viktor Lowenfeld, an Austrian-born art educator, made a significant impact on art therapy in the art education field. Lowenfeld considered a child's artwork to be indicative of developing abilities in motor skills, perception, language, symbol formation, sensory awareness, and spatial orientation (Malchiodi, 1998). In 1947, his book *Creative and Mental Growth* described his art theory of child artistic development in six distinct stages. Art therapists have relied on these stages to inform their analyses of a child's responses during assessment and to the development of treatment planning (Malchiodi, 2011). These stages helped to identify what artistic skills children and adolescents can achieve at various stages of development. By knowing where children's abilities can be artistically and at what age, art therapists identified possible developmental delays and how that impacted them in daily life.

Florence Cane is another important figure who made contributions to art education and the field of art therapy. She was Margaret Naumberg's sister and worked as an art educator at the Walden School. Her method was to teach art to her students in a way that provided an outlet for them to express who they were. In 1951, she wrote *The Artist in Each of Us*, and included exercises and techniques to use in the classroom to nurture the inner artists of all students. One such exercise that art therapists use to this day is called the "scribble technique," used to reduce any inhibitions of art-making and facilitate spontaneous imagery from the unconscious (Cane, 1951). Cane's approach has been used to help students develop and grow not only as art students but in life.

1.4   Progression of the Art Therapy Field

Since the 1950s, the development of the field has progressed, and art therapy has been applied to other human development theories such as Cognitive-Behavioral, Gestalt, Humanistic, and Adlerian. More key figures and pioneers contributed to showcasing the benefits of using art therapy through published articles, texts, and research. The establishment of the American Art Therapy Association (AATA) took place in 1969, and since then has been advancing the field, improving the educational standards for art therapy training, and honoring art therapists who have made significant contributions to the field through the Honorary Life Member (HLM) Award (AATA, 1993). As mentioned in the introduction, one such key figure was Harriet Wadeson, an HLM named in 1992 by the AATA for her contribution to the field. In addition to establishing one of the first art therapy graduate programs in the Midwest at the University of Illinois at Chicago (UIC), she has authored 8 art therapy books, over 70 articles in professional journals, and served on the board of AATA (UIC Today, 2016). As I mentioned in the introduction, I had the privilege of attending her graduate art therapy program at UIC, the first in Chicago, which ran for 24 years (UIC Today, 2016).

As part of Wadeson's Art Therapy Graduate Program, I learned to combine the creative process of art-making with the therapeutic process while working as an intern with patients hospitalized in the psychiatric unit at one placement site, and working with adolescents at-risk of dropping out of high school at another. I practiced through the lens of Wadeson's approach to art therapy characterized as "eclectic," allowing for openness to multiple theories while integrating a multicultural perspective. In Wadeson's later years, she revisited this eclectic approach and described the approach to include areas of trauma, its physiological effects, and the larger community (Wadeson, 2016). This eclectic approach has been the root of my work in integrating art therapy approaches in school counselings and will be described throughout this book.

1.5   Art Therapy and Neuroscience

In more recent years, advances in neuroscience have helped to explain the impact of art and the art-making process on the brain and the mind-body connection.

These findings help to understand how creating art has de-stressing abilities, as well as the ability to retrieve memories.

In 2016, Kaimal G., Ray K, and Muniz J. led a study on the effects of creating art on stress. Cortisol levels were measured to depict stress among 39 adult participants by taking their saliva samples. The research found that there was a significant decrease in the levels of cortisol after the session. The participants also shared qualitative data, describing the session as relaxing, free, and insightful (Kaimal et al., 2016). These outcomes were not influenced by the age or gender of participants, nor whether or not they identified as someone with art experience (Kaimal et al., 2016). In another study, King et al. (2017) compared brain activity, specifically cortical activation patterns, by collecting electroencephalogram or EEG levels of 10 adults with no major medical conditions immediately after art-making and rote motor tasks, such as coin tossing and pencil rotation. Significant and distinct differences were observed post-art making compared to completing rote motor tasks. Though more research can be done in the areas of art-making and stress-relieving qualities, these findings may explain why so many educators, whether school counselors or not, have offered students to create art as a means to de-escalate from stressful experiences.

Neuroscience has also helped to explain how memories are stored in visual form in the brain, making the case of why creating images through art to recall memories, including traumatic memories, is much more accessible than through written or verbal means. Knowing that the process of creating art and how it impacts parts of the brain is particularly helpful in applying trauma-informed practices. Studies have found that when a person has gone through the survival response after a trauma has occurred, the experience is remembered in fragments and images rather than in words (Tinnin & Gantt, 2013 as cited in Walker, 2020). Accordingly, drawing is hypothesized to facilitate verbal reports of these underlying emotionally charged events. Once a memory is retrieved through art, this helps an individual organize narratives and provide more details than if an interview relied solely on verbal or written attempts to communicate these experiences (Gross & Hayne, 1998). Cathy Malchiodi (1997/2001), as cited in Malchiodi (2012), observed this in working as an art therapist with children from violent homes. Creating art helped them connect emotions with stressful events, providing a way to make sense of what happened to them, leading to learning ways to cope (Malchiodi, 1997/2001 as cited in Malchiodi, 2012). The rationale of integrating art therapy approaches as a trauma-informed practice in school counseling will be discussed further in Chapter 2.

1.6 Application of Art Therapy

With the psychoanalytic origins, translation into education, and advances in neuroscience highlighting the positive effects of art and art-making on stress and memory, people from all walks of life can benefit from art therapy. Art's restorative and healing power has helped address a wide range of mental health challenges, no matter the age, gender, race, cultural background, and personal experiences, and in a wide variety of settings. We will now look at the benefits of applying art therapy to different populations: adults, children, and adolescents.

1.7   Art Therapy with Adults

Though this book is specifically for those working with grades Pre-Kindergarten through 12th-grade students, it's important to highlight the benefits to adults to demonstrate how art therapy meets the needs of so many people, no matter their age. Contrary to what many may believe about art therapy, art therapy is beneficial to adults just as much as it is to children. To this day, art therapy is provided to adults in numerous settings, nursing homes, outpatient mental health centers, domestic violence shelters, private practices, homeless shelters, and community centers. In Chapter 6, I will describe my experience as a school counseling specialist, integrating art therapy approaches in providing professional development to school counselors districtwide.

My first job was working in a hospital, where I provided short-term art therapy groups for adults who were hospitalized and stayed in the inpatient psychiatric or substance abuse units, anywhere from a few days to a few weeks. They were patients who either had a diagnosis of depression, bipolar disorder, schizophrenia, substance abuse disorder, or dual diagnosis of a mental health and substance abuse disorder. During their time in the hospital, I provided art therapy as a means to decrease the symptoms of illness, such as anxiety and severe depression, as well as from being in an unfamiliar place with people they did not know.

Whenever I entered the unit, the patients who saw me for the first time with my art supplies balked at the idea of having to participate in a "kid's activity." However, once I was able to convince them to keep an open mind and let them know if they didn't feel comfortable participating at any time, they did not have to. When provided with simple materials, such as oil pastels and multi-media paper, along with jazz or classical music in the background, the opportunity to create art among others who were going through the same struggles offered a sense of connection. The interesting part of facilitating art with adults as opposed to children and adolescents is that they've had more time to master working around their words or talking themselves out of accepting their current reality. This hiding behind their words helped to avoid the difficult work of talking about their feelings and being vulnerable to others. Understandably in their current circumstances, emotions can be overwhelming and scary, but expressing them through art can be a less fearful route. Much of what was represented in their individual art was apparent in other group members' art. This commonality found through their art helped them to relate to one another, opening up a discussion about meaning in their actions, which appeared especially helpful for those who were hospitalized for substance abuse. With the support of others' in the group, they could recognize the harm in their choices, while also acknowledging that the process of change is hard, yet not impossible. The sharing of art among the group members seemed to provide relief as they realized that they were not alone in their struggles. I often saw patients leaving the session happy with what they worked on and wanting to keep their art. It was rewarding to see the progress they've made toward the end of their stay in the hospital, expressing appreciation for the support they've received to be able to go back home.

Besides my professional experience with adults, there continues to be more research on the efficacy of art therapy with adults, as the need for quantifiable results is used for funding for treatment. One example of the effectiveness of art therapy with adults is provided through a study of art therapy as a treatment for women diagnosed with generalized anxiety disorder, with moderate to severe anxiety symptoms. Abbing et al. (2019) implemented this study of 47 women aged 18–65 years old who participated in 10–12 individual art therapy sessions of 45–60 minutes for three months. During this time, participants worked on free art and other art directives that aligned with their treatment goals. Results of the study found that compared to participants on a waiting list to receive treatment, these participants experienced a reduction in anxiety, an increase in subjective quality of life, and an improvement in accessing strategies to regulate emotions (Abbing et al., 2019). Studies such as these can affirm the benefits of art therapy with adults, as much as they are to children and adolescents.

1.8   Art Therapy with Children

Art therapy with children has been applied in various settings to address different stressors and challenges that are prevalent in childhood, especially those that impact well-being, mental and physical health, growth, and development. Art is attractive to children, with its playful nature and freedom to express oneself. The early developmental years are where creating art appears to be most encouraged, whether this is at home, school, daycare, or while waiting in the doctor's office. Therefore, it seems only natural to apply art-making in the therapeutic process. This also addresses any communication and comprehension limitations, as children are still in the process of developing their speech and language abilities.

Right before becoming a school counselor, I worked for a community service agency where I provided therapy to children who were formerly part of the foster care system and had recently been adopted, most often by a family member. Many of the presenting areas of need for these children were trauma from abuse or neglect by biological parents, feelings of rejection and anger, difficulty adjusting to their new homes, and issues with trust and attachment. These stressors manifested in their behaviors, whether at home or at school, either lashing out at their adoptive parents or their teachers physically or verbally, destroying things at home, or stealing family members' belongings. On the other hand, some children internalized their feelings toward their situation through self-injurious behavior. As these children were assigned to my caseload, I introduced the art-making process as a means to build trust, as understandably, they had lost trust in the very adults who were supposed to protect them. Creating imagery for them was a small step toward being able to communicate and have an outlet to express emotions that overwhelmed them daily. Using something they created on their own, through an encouraging non-judgmental atmosphere, was one way to relieve symptoms that led to harmful behaviors, and unpack the overwhelming and traumatic experiences they've endured in their young lives. This helped to create a path to trust, feeling secure, and recognizing their resilience.

A review of research and methods used to establish art therapy as a treatment for children with trauma found that it was an effective treatment across various settings and applications (Eaton et al., 2007). Eaton et al reviewed studies with participant demographics including children aged 5 to 11, with some adolescents aged 12–17, who either had no diagnosis or had diagnoses such as Post-traumatic Stress Disorder (PTSD), chronic depression, or conduct disorder. These participants received art therapy as a treatment method for childhood trauma after tragic events such as the terrorist attacks on 9/11 at the World Trade Center, exposure to war violence, gun violence in the community, or the loss of a loved one. Art therapy treatment varied from weeks to months, resulting in a reduction of anxiety, reduced PTSD symptoms based on pre- and post-change scores, and increased awareness in the child's understanding of their diagnoses (Eaton et al., 2007).

In addition to studies, there have been a multitude of text publications on the efficacy of art therapy and working with children. Judith Rubin, who was known as the "Art Lady" on the beloved television series "Mister Rogers Neighborhood" showcased art projects with children in the late 1960s (*Remembering Mister Rogers*, n.d.). Rubin went on to write a classic reference for mental health professionals who use art therapy with children titled *Child Art Therapy*, originally written in 1978 and updated in the 25th Anniversary edition. It provides case studies spanning Rubin's career as an art therapist and provides insight into children's experiences in art therapy sessions. Rubin illustrates conditions for creative growth, and the use of art in individual, group, and family therapy settings among others. These children were faced with a diverse set of challenges, from those who were diagnosed with schizophrenia in a psychiatric hospital to others with physical disabilities in a residential institution.

One chapter entitled, "Helping the Normal Child through Art," (Rubin, 2005, pp. 311–329) focuses on the therapeutic nature of artwork produced in an art education classroom. This chapter highlights how students can benefit from art therapy, whether or not they were diagnosed with a mental health disorder, identified as having a disability, or have gone through a significant amount of trauma. Rubin describes cases of students whose feelings and behaviors manifested in their artwork made in art class that represented their internal experiences undetectable from the outside, that had the potential to impact their learning. This came in many forms throughout their art, from the student who expressed distress from losing their bike, to another student who got in trouble with a parent before school, or to the student who was grieving the loss of a parent. Rubin emphasized that teachers often are the first people in a child's life to see and hear about stressful events, and they establish a strong, consistent relationship with the child from seeing them daily. From this, the use of art and its effectiveness in facilitating support and intervention where needed demonstrates the value of art in a school setting. In Chapter 4, we will explore ways for school counselors to collaborate with art teachers to facilitate the use of art in learning and for its therapeutic potential.

1.9   Art Therapy with Adolescents

Art therapy with adolescents is effective in addressing the trials and tribulations of this unique stage in life. My first time working with adolescents came through an art therapy internship at a non-profit social service agency housed within a public high school. It was here that I met with students struggling academically and at risk of dropping out of school altogether. Many of the students referred to art therapy came from single-parent, low-income households, while living in a neighborhood plagued with gang violence in recent decades. This is where I saw firsthand that students were coming in with reading skills equivalent to 3 or 4 levels below the grade level they were currently enrolled, yet no academic interventions were in place at the time, only a referral to see me, an art therapy intern. I slowly recognized the flaws of a much bigger system, yet I needed to gain perspective of their lived experiences in high school and life.

Many times, the goal was to help students identify who they were in this huge system that did not seem to be set up for their success. As part of my internship, I had the opportunity to join a special education art class once a week and provide art therapy to 9th-grade students. I designed my lessons to enhance identity development among Latino students to increase self-awareness and self-esteem. I implemented art directives, such as handmade doll-making, self-identity flags, and collages, to emphasize and celebrate each of their unique traits. In their self-identity flags, students showcased their cultural backgrounds, demonstrating pride in their Puerto Rican or Mexican roots.

Drawing on research, a notable study of the use of art therapy with adolescents was found to have a positive change on the participants' identity development (Kelemen & Shamri-Zeevi, 2022). The study evaluates the impact of an open art studio designed to help adolescents in a therapeutic day school. The students at this school were not able to attend a traditional mainstream school due to mental health conditions, resulting in truancy or hospitalization. These students lost significant interaction with peers, which had a severe impact on their identity development. The participants in the study had the opportunity to participate in the open art studio to create and express themselves through the art materials with limited instruction; there was no pressure to share their art, and there was ample time and space to work quietly. The art therapists were there to support their growth as they learned about themselves through their art. At the end of the ten month process, the study found remarkable levels of recovery through their art or changes in behavior. For example, one adolescent who had been separated from their peers was able to gain self-confidence, felt reduced social anxiety, and had increased willingness to interact with their peers again. Though more research is needed, the use of art therapy in a safe and supportive environment can facilitate the healthy development of identity among adolescents.

1.10   Application of Art Therapy in School Districts

As mentioned previously, art therapy has been applied in a variety of settings as a treatment method to address mental health and well-being. For the purpose of this text and in relation to school counselors and other mental health professionals working in the school setting, we will take a look at the implementation of art therapy in the education system.

While there has been art therapy provided in individual schools through a variety of ways, such as through community mental health centers partnering with that school, or art educators integrating therapeutic approaches in their teaching practice, there seems to be less integration of art therapy at the district level. As art therapy in schools gained attention since the start of the art therapy field, there have been a few districts that have integrated it at the district level, making it accessible to a larger number of students.

In the United States, the Miami-Dade County Public Schools (M-DCPS) is perhaps one of the first to implement art therapy as a school district, making it accessible to students receiving special education services. This program began as a pilot program in 1979 to assist students' emotional functioning and increase their academic involvement (Isis et al., 2010). It was probably the only established program in a school system at that time and to this day, M-DCPS is the largest employer of art therapists in the United States. There is a system in place for students to be referred to art therapy services in the form of individual and small group art therapy sessions for students identified with emotional/behavioral disabilities (Isis et al., 2010). These students have goals written per their Individual Education Plan (IEP) to address social, emotional, and cognitive skills, to enhance their learning.

One of the strategies that the M-DCPS art therapy program implemented addressed students' anxiety during high-stakes standardized testing time. During this time of the school year, students displayed an increase of maladaptive behaviors and psychiatric hospitalizations. In response, art therapy allowed the students an opportunity to depict fears, concerns, and feelings related to the high-stakes exam. From there, art therapists led them in developing positive affirmations related to their imagery, and in lieu of creating a written to do list, art therapists facilitated the creation of a visual of test-taking strategies for students to refer to. Finally, students created journals documenting subjects, hobbies, and activities that made them feel successful. Having this artwork was helpful to revisit skills learned through the art-making process. As a result of these services, accompanied with educating students about IEP accommodations and test-taking skills, the number of maladaptive incidents that occurred during the testing season previously was reduced (Isis et al., 2010).

Another school district that has an established art therapy program is the New York University Art Therapy in Schools Program. It is available to general education students who need support with emotional and behavioral challenges. This program also started as a pilot in two public schools that were in close proximity to the 9/11 attacks. It proved to be effective, which resulted in its expansion in Chinatown, where art therapy was found to align with the community's values (Berberian & Davis, 2020). With local, federal, and private donor funding, the program continues to serve students struggling in NYC (Berberian & Davis, 2020). The program is designed to be proactive and preventive, providing free, accessible treatment services in the school setting for general education students struggling emotionally and behaviorally (Berberian & Davis, 2020). The program's model has an established referral process from teachers and other school staff members, allowing for immediate assessment and response services through art therapy (Berberian & Davis, 2020).

Outside of the United States, what is notable is that in almost every educational setting in Israel, art therapists are employed to support students' integration into school, making art therapy accessible for the purpose of increasing their abilities to learn and participate in social activities (Snir, 2022). In an effort to examine the impact of art therapy and its success on treatment outcomes, Snir (2022) facilitated a longitudinal study over the span of two years to examine the relationship between artmaking in art therapy sessions and the child's experiences in the school environment. The participants in the study received special education services in one form or another, did not receive any other type of therapeutic treatment outside of school art therapy, and were referred for social/ emotional difficulties, low self-esteem, and other factors affecting their ability to learn (Snir, 2022). The results of the study highlighted a connection between positive artmaking experiences and improvements in internalizing issues, somatic problems, depression, and anxiety (Snir, 2022).

Finally, at the time of writing this book, I am conducting a small pilot study with 8 school counselors working at different schools in the district. Through providing training, providing art materials, ongoing consultation, and community of practice meetings, school counselors in this cohort are implementing art therapy integrated small group sessions. Preliminary quantitative and qualitative data that demonstrate the impact on students' ability to learn the American School Counselor Association (ASCA) Standards and increase academic achievement appear positive. Case studies from these small groups will be discussed throughout this book.

Up until this point, I've gone through the foundation of art therapy, art therapy with adults, children, and adolescents, and art therapy in school settings. Before heading into the next chapter that will align art therapy with meeting the Ethical Standards of the ASCA, I felt it was important to go over some common misconceptions about art therapy. Misconceptions of the field could serve as a barrier to students having the opportunity to access art through services already established in the school, such as school counseling.

1.11   Common Misconceptions of Art Therapy

Once we debunk some common myths, we can fully embrace why integrating art therapy approaches can be beneficial to school counselors and, in turn, the students. We can then explain our methods to key team members such as administration, teachers, and parents to garner support from the school community, not only for our role but for the benefit of embracing the arts in schools.

1   *"You have to be a good artist to participate in art therapy."*
    Unlike art education, the goal is not to master artistic skills nor to achieve aesthetic value. Rather it is about the process, and what the art means to the artist for self-awareness, expression, and well-being.
2   *"Art therapy is only for clinical, long-term psychotherapy."*
    Art therapy draws upon several counseling theories that many school counselors use, such as solution-focused brief therapy, cognitive behavioral, Adlerian, and person-centered. Whichever theoretical orientation is used, the efficiency of art therapy to help students express themselves in a shorter time period through their art, while experiencing the de-stressing qualities that traditional "talk therapy" does not offer, makes for seamless integration of art therapy approaches in school counseling practice.
3   *"Art therapy is only beneficial to younger, elementary school students."*
    Art therapy is beneficial for all ages. Once given the autonomy and encouragement to create freely without worrying about what their art would look like, anyone can benefit from the self-growth and healing properties of art therapy.
4   *"Art Therapy is used to psychoanalyze a person's art and uncover certain meanings."*
    While art therapy is rooted in psychoanalysis, art is used to help a person interpret the meaning of their own art. The art therapist can help someone process their art by asking clarifying questions about their art and inquiring about what they think and feel about the process and their final art product.
5   *"Coloring pages are a form of art therapy."*
    While I have used coloring pages with students, I don't consider this an art therapy approach. It can be soothing to fill in spaces with color, and the result

can be aesthetically pleasing. Art therapy draws upon much more, including building rapport with the therapist, identifying meaning in their art, making connections with others through art, and increasing self-awareness and self-identity, as art can be seen as the extension of self. Coloring in a pre-defined image may also encourage the notion of what a person's art should look like. With an art therapy approach, creating art allows for much more freedom, and embracing the final art product, no matter what it looks like.

1.12 Building on Foundation

In this chapter, we have explored the foundation of art therapy, its origin and key figures, its application among diverse populations, including the school setting, and common misconceptions. In Chapter 2, we will dive deeper into *how* integrating art therapy approaches into school counseling practice aligns with the ASCA Ethical Standards to provide equitable, culturally responsive, and trauma-informed support to students.

References

Abbing, A., Baars, E. W., De Sonneville, L., Ponstein, A. S., & Swaab, H. (2019). The effectiveness of art therapy for anxiety in adult women: A randomized controlled trial. *Frontiers in Psychology*, *10*, 1203. https://doi.org/10.3389/fpsyg.2019.01203

About the American Art Therapy Association. (2023, January 18). American Art Therapy Association. https://arttherapy.org/about/

Adrian Hill, UK founder of Art Therapy by Morgan Bush, Intern. (n.d.). https://arttherapycentre.com/blog/adrian-hill-uk-founder-art-therapy-morgan-bush-intern/

American Art Therapy Association Honorary Life Member Award -Harriet Wadeson, PhD, A.T.R., HLM. (1993). Art Therapy. *Journal of the American Art Therapy Association*, *10*(1), 10–13. https://doi.org/https://doi.org/10.1080/07421656.1993.10758971

Berberian, M., & Davis, B. (2020). *Art therapy practices for resilient youth: A strengths-based approach to at-promise children and adolescents*. Routledge.

Bitonte, R. A., & De Santo, M. (2014). Art therapy: An underutilized, yet effective tool. *Mental Illness*, *6*(1), 18–19. https://doi.org/10.4081/mi.2014.5354

Cane, F. (1951). *The artist in each of us*. Pantheon Books.

Dewey, J. (1958). *Art as experience*. London: Putnam.

Eaton, L. G., Doherty, K. L., & Widrick, R. M. (2007). A review of research and methods used to establish art therapy as an effective treatment method for traumatized children. *The Arts in Psychotherapy*, *34*, 256–262.

Gross, J., & Hayne, H. (1998). Drawing facilitates children's verbal reports of emotionally laden events. *Journal of Experimental Psychology Applied*, *4*(2), 163–179. https://doi.org/10.1037/1076-898x.4.2.163

Isis, P. D., Bush, J., Siegel, C. A., & Ventura, Y. (2010). Empowering students through creativity: Art therapy in Miami-Dade County public schools. *Art Therapy*, *27*(2), 56–61. https://doi.org/10.1080/07421656.2010.10129712

Junge, M. B. (2016). History of art therapy. In D. E. Gusak & M. L. Rosal (Eds.), *The wiley handbook of art therapy* (pp. 7–16). John Wiley & Sons, Ltd.

Junge, M. B., & Asawa, P. P. (1994). *A history of art therapy in the United States.* American Art Therapy Association.

Kaimal, G., Ray, K., & Muniz, J. (2016). Reduction of cortisol levels and participants' responses following art making. *Art Therapy, 33*(2), 74–80. https://doi.org/10.1080/07421656.2016.1166832

Kelemen, L. J., & Shamri-Zeevi, L. (2022). Art therapy open studio and teen identity development: Helping adolescents recover from mental health conditions. *Children, 9*(7), 1029. https://doi.org/10.3390/children9071029

King, J. L. (2017). Cortical activity changes after art making and rote motor movement as measured by EEG: A preliminary study. *Biomedical Journal of Scientific & Technical Research, 1*(4), 1062–1075. https://doi.org/10.26717/bjstr.2017.01.000366

Lowenfeld, V., & Brittain, W. L. (1987). *Creative and mental growth.* Prentice Hall.

Malchiodi C. A. (1997). *Breaking the silence: Art therapy with children from violent homes.* New York: Brunner/Mazel.

Malchiodi, C. A. (1998). *Understanding children's drawings.* Guilford Publications. https://eric.ed.gov/?id=ED422114

Malchiodi, C. A. (2011). *Handbook of art therapy* (2nd ed.). Guilford Publications. https://eric.ed.gov/?id=ED535953

Malchioldi, C. A. (2012). Art therapy and the brain. In C. A. Malchioldi (Ed.), *Handbook of art therapy* (pp. 16–24). The Guilford Press.

Margaret Naumburg. (n.d.). Jewish Women's Archive. https://jwa.org/encyclopedia/article/naumburg-margaret

Remembering Mister Rogers. (n.d.). Kansas City PBS. https://www.kansascitypbs.org/highlights/remembering-mister-rogers-dr-judy-rubin-reflects-time-art-lady/

Rubin, J. A. (2005). *Child art therapy.* John Wiley & Sons, Inc.

Snir, S. (2022). Artmaking in elementary school art therapy: Associations with pre-treatment behavioral problems and therapy outcomes. *Children, 9*(9), 1277. https://doi.org/10.3390/children9091277

Tinnin, M.D, & Gantt, L. (2013). *The instinctual trauma response & dual-brain dynamics: A guide for trauma therapy.* Gargoyle Press.

UIC News staff. (n.d.). Deaths: Harriet Wadeson. *UIC today.* https://today.uic.edu/deaths-harriet-wadeson/

Vick, R. M. (2003). A brief history of art therapy. In C. A. Malchioldi (Ed.), *Handbook of art therapy* (pp. 5–15). The Guilford Press.

Wadeson, H. (2016). An eclectic approach to art therapy - revisited. In D. E. Gusak & M. L. Rosal (Eds.), *The wiley handbook of art therapy* (pp. 122–131). John Wiley & Sons, Ltd.

Walker, M. K. (2020). "My passed!!!" A case study of the efficacy of art therapy with adolescents with complex trauma and attachment disruptions. In M. Berberian & B. Davis (Eds.), *Art therapy practices for resilient youth: A strengths-based approach to at-promise children and adolescents* (pp. 425–442). Routledge.

Chapter 2

Art Therapy Approaches for Equitable and Trauma-Informed School Counseling

Alignment with the American School Counseling Association Ethical Standards

2.1 Art Therapy Integration: An Equitable Approach to Reach All Students

As schools are often the first place where children and adolescents exhibit symptoms and behaviors that impact well-being and, in turn, academic achievement, school counselors are well-positioned to address these issues as soon as they are apparent. However, with an increased number of student referrals for behavioral health, attendance, and other issues impacting academic achievement comes an increase in diversity, as learning styles and other needs are wide and varied. School counseling practice is built on the foundation of being accessible to everyone. So, how can this be made possible?

The American School Counselor Association set forth the ASCA Ethical Standards for School Counselors, which outline the "principles of ethical behavior necessary to maintain the highest standards of integrity, leadership, and professionalism" (American School Counselor Association, 2022). Interwoven throughout the ASCA Ethical Standards, you can see key themes of equity, such as respecting and affirming a student's identity, protecting them from harm, and ensuring access to services inclusive of their cultural background, experiences, and all that encompasses who they are. As such, school counselors play a critical role in educational equity by acknowledging the differences among students, identifying inequities in resources and opportunities, and creating a plan to address these disparities to ensure all students are set up for success (American School Counselor Association, 2022). These standards state that equity is at the forefront of a school counselor's practice so that students from all backgrounds and circumstances are supported in a physically safe and inclusive environment (ASCA, 2022). Additionally, the ethical responsibility of school counselors includes

advocating and affirming all students regardless of but not limited to ethnic/racial identity; nationality; age; social class; economic status; abilities/disabilities;

DOI: 10.4324/9781003430940-4

language; immigration status; sexual orientation; gender identity; gender expression; family type; religious/spiritual identity; and living situations, including emancipated minor status, wards of the state, homelessness or incarceration.

(ASCA, 2022, p. 1)

Educational equity is at the forefront of a school counselor's work when they strive to ensure that every student receives what they need to develop their full academic, social, and emotional potential despite race, gender ethnicity, language, disability, family background, or family income (Srinivasan, 2019). In my role as a school counseling specialist, much of my work in recent years has been focused on equity, ensuring that school counselors are champions of this mission in the school building. With the recent light shed on inequities due to systemic racism, and the global pandemic exacerbating these inequities, there is a call to action for school counselors now more than ever. It is important to acknowledge the disparities that exist for our marginalized youth, whether it be a lack of mental health resources in the community, the arts, sports, education, or role models that look like them going on to college or rewarding careers. This eventually shows up in schools as students with a lack of access to resources, compared to their counterparts, are farthest from being on track to graduating high school. A school counselor plays a significant role in making sure students have just as much of an opportunity to succeed as those from more resourced backgrounds. So how could art therapy approaches help school counselors meet these standards and best serve students with an equity lens?

As mentioned in Chapter 1, the influence of art therapy in art education came about to understand the whole child. Providing the opportunity for students to express themselves through art capitalizes on a period when our youth are still developing, learning, exploring, and growing as people who will become our future. Introducing ways for them to discover and appreciate who they are, and for others to do so as well, can make for an inclusive environment that affirms the belonging of all students. In turn, it helps them to maximize their academic potential. While introducing art therapy approaches into practice will not resolve all factors contributing to inequity, we can make the most out of its benefits regardless of culture, economic status, language, gender, and so on, to foster learning and growth for all students.

In this chapter, we will look closer at how using art therapy approaches ensures equitable outcomes where students' needs are met with care and respect for who they are, adhering to the ASCA Ethical Standards. These approaches support academic success and foster the social-emotional skills necessary for career readiness and lifelong learning for an increasingly diverse student population, setting them up for success beyond high school graduation. The importance of interweaving both culturally responsiveness and trauma-informed practices as a means to provide equitable school counseling services will also be highlighted.

2.2   School Counseling with an Equity Lens

At the time of writing this book, I am serving as a school counseling specialist supporting school counselors across a large, urban, midwestern school district through professional development, coaching, and consultation. At the beginning of one school year, many school counselors reported needing guidance on effective practice to meet the needs of an unprecedented influx of newcomer student enrollment, or foreign-born students who recently arrived in the US. Counselors expressed feeling overwhelmed with the lack of resources and training available to meet their needs. In many schools, there hadn't been students in need of English Language Learner (ELL) support until the newcomer students' recent arrival, leaving them with no one in the building who (1) can speak to them in their native language and (2) had a certification to teach ELL students. In addition to the language barrier, newcomer students and families needed basic resources, such as food and clothing. School counselors reported that students lacked the proper attire to commute to school in cold weather, making attendance inconsistent. Many were living in temporary living conditions, moving from police stations to shelters temporarily, then on to another location until they could find permanent housing. This instability, combined with students' lack of basic resources, resulted in school attendance far lower than their peers.

All the while adjusting to their new environment, underlying was the trauma from pre-migration experiences. The lack of mental health resources in the community to meet the needs of students and families led to school counselors becoming the main resource to address mental health. Considering the amount of trauma that these students were going through pre- and post-migration, it was clear to many counselors that this had to be addressed if there was any hope for them to become adjusted to their entirely new world, let alone the school setting. And for the latter, some newcomer students experienced a less-than-warm welcome from their peers. School counselors reported tension between newcomer students and other student groups. Overall, the newcomer students have become some of the most vulnerable in the school district, and school counselors wanted to help them.

School counselors were putting equity into action as with the case of the newcomer students, bringing awareness to the discrepancy of resources compared to other students. Several factors were considered to see how large the gap was in being able to succeed in school – limited basic resources, language barrier, cultural differences, cultural assimilation, and past and ongoing traumatic experiences. Though the ability to close this gap comes from different parts of the educational system coming together, the intentional use of art with students who are at a disadvantage can at least be the beginning of connection and healing.

2.3   Art Therapy Integration: A Tool for Equity

Art is a universal language. The use of art in a school setting by school counselors draws upon a language that transcends limitations of verbal communication abilities, and language and cultural barriers. Art can be the medium in which students can express their needs, share their worries, and showcase their interests in a safe and non-threatening environment. So, when school counselors brought their concern about the ability to meet the needs of newcomers to the district school counseling department's attention, I couldn't help but think about art.

In my experience as a school counselor, integrating art therapy into my practice helped to connect with students no matter their first language, nor their written or verbal abilities. Often students were referred to me who had difficulty with reading, writing, math, or all the core subjects, coupled with behavior challenges in the classroom and little to no participation in class. When provided the opportunity to create art, I observed that using the art as a reference can provide another means for students to express their strengths. Through the student's art, I recognized that students do have communication skills, and using art as their vehicle makes it possible. Additionally, they could use it to analyze and problem-solve. Creating art removes the need to do math, write, or read, and allows students a different way to showcase their analytical skills and ability to think critically. As a result, they can reflect on their art and interpret it for others in the group, to the counselor, or in a classroom.

2.4   Seeing Is Believing

With the ability to analyze their art comes an opportunity to gain a deeper understanding of self and the world surrounding them. Every time a student enters the school building, they bring their entire ecosystem – the neighborhood they live in, their family expectations, society's perception of them, and their self-perception. School counselors and educators alike should have a strong belief in students' ability to succeed no matter their ecosystem, however, if the students don't believe the same, any efforts to help them on a path to success after high school are futile.

So what can school counselors do? By promoting what Paolo Freire (2005, as cited in Keane, 2017) calls "critical consciousness," students can "reflect deeply about themselves concerning their social climate, explore inherent contradictions in those relationships, and become empowered to problem-solve." When students recognize what factors impact their education, they can pave the way for a future they want to see for themselves. As they are allowed to liberate themselves from preconceived notions of their future, they can set up a plan to overcome any barriers. For example, when students learn about the history of systemic racism, they can decide to persevere and address challenges that were set up before they even started school, and create their own visual narrative to achieve success. This can be seen from Figure 2.1, where a student created art to visualize receiving a scholarship for college.

A visual of themselves in the future also serves to close-the-gap on the lack of role models they see every day that look like them. Marian Edelman Wright (2021), founder of the Children's Defense Fund, believed that children needed visible role models to be inspired by their future. She took a stance on how books still lack a diversity of characters and subject matter that children of color can relate to. In addition to books, school is another space where students of color will not see adult figures they can relate to, impacting their own beliefs of achieving academically and thinking about their futures (Zirkel, 2002). While the student population in public schools has become more racially and ethnically diverse, the public school teacher population is less so. The National Center for Education Statistics (2020) reported that White and non-Hispanic elementary and secondary public school teachers made up 79% of the population. At the same time, in schools where the majority of students were not White, the majority of teachers tended to be White. The majority of teachers were White in schools where a majority of students were Hispanic (54%), Black (54%), Asian (60%), or American Indian/Alaska Native (61%) (National Center for Education Statistics, 2020). In other words, a larger percentage of teachers were White than of the same race/ethnicity as the majority of students (National Center for Education Statistics, 2020).

Figure 2.1 A student's drawing of his future self, graduating and receiving a college scholarship.

The lack of role models who look like the students does not have to limit the possibilities and opportunities they can have for a promising future. A school counselor can act as an agent for change and disrupt the negative impact of a lack of role models. By exploring the possibilities through art, students have the opportunity to create themselves as the main characters in their success stories. This can be seen in Figure 2.3, where students were encouraged to draw themselves in their dream career. Providing this art directive to students was a first step in helping them envision and believe they can have a promising future. From there, school counselors can implement interventions, resources, and programming with intent to help students gain hope and a mindset to help them move forward and succeed. For the student who is worried that their parents can't afford college, we teach them how scholarships work along with other financial aid opportunities. For the student who would be the first in their family to go to college, we can provide the knowledge and skills to pick a postsecondary institution that meets their academic needs, career aspirations, financial situation, and any other factors that contribute to the best fit for the student.

What needs to be highlighted in using art as a tool for equity is how it addresses multiple factors that contribute to promoting an equitable educational space for students. With the case of the newcomer students, along with other student populations who have been historically under-resourced, it is important to recognize the need to be culturally responsive and trauma-informed in our practices, to achieve equitable access to services.

2.5   The Culturally Responsive School Counselor and Art Therapy

As a district school counseling specialist, I have the opportunity to visit many elementary, middle, and high schools throughout the city. Upon entering a school building, I immediately notice visual cues of whether it is inclusive of a diverse student population. Signs such as "You Belong," and "I am an Undocumented Student Ally," as well as LGBTQ+ flags and flags representing different countries, schools have already embraced the visual impact of a welcoming environment for students. This type of environment is crucial as many students come into the school building with numerous stressors already – constraints of society, the stigma on mental health, ostracization by the community based on their gender identity, and the influence of social media. The last thing we want is a school environment that exacerbates these stressors even more. But, how can school counselors act on this and expand on the impact of visuals on a positive, inclusive school environment?

Within the call to achieve educational equity, there is a need to affirm all cultures, as it is a pervasive and influential factor, and as a response to the cultural diversification in schools and communities (American School Counselor Association, 2021). This may seem like a tall order for school counselors to be able to learn all about the different cultural backgrounds of their student population. But there is a simple, effective way to achieve this, and it starts with art. The idea is to allow the students to tell you about themselves. As long as they are provided with the opportunity to do so in a safe environment, students can showcase who they, deterring stereotypes and implicit bias. This aligns with the concept of multiculturalism, embracing the coexistence of diverse cultural groups within a society. Art has the ability to recognize and value the richness and contributions of different cultural backgrounds (Al-Zadjali, 2024).

2.6   Cultural Competence and Art: A Closer Look

A few years ago, while cleaning out my parents' old home, I came across a report card from my Kindergarten year. The teacher wrote that my class participation was satisfactory, though if I would only talk, I would do much better in school. Thinking back, I believe I had symptoms of selective mutism. I have some visual memories of that year, none of which include talking to any of my classmates or my teacher. I remember being confused as to why there were so many kids around and why they were all so loud. I didn't utter a word to anyone, and I sat off to the side by myself during carpet time. I wasn't used to a whole lot of talking and expression and playing and jumping about. Growing up, I remember my mother instilling in me to not call too much attention to myself, stay quiet and humble, and speak only when I have something to say. This was a value as an immigrant from the Philippines, which she has come to know as having a positive impact on life overall. Looking back, I must have felt overwhelmed and alone. I should add that there was only one other Asian student in the class; the rest of my classmates were White.

Fast forward to today, I can't help but wonder how my experience would have been different had there been knowledge and understanding of the impact of cultural values on my experience in school. Currently, it does appear that we have a way to go in education. Let's take, for example, students who have a cultural background rooted in Eastern philosophies that value modesty and being quiet. When these same students attend a school where being vocal and asserting one's needs are associated with positive characteristic traits such as being intellectual and having leadership skills, these students are then seen as "passive" and "non-communicators" (Li et al., 2010). In a study of Chinese immigrant children in predominantly White or European American students and staff, Li et al. (2010) found that these children had more school adjustment problems and negative relationships with learning and friends according to teacher reports. In contrast, in Asian-dominant preschools in the US located in Asian-dominant neighborhoods, teachers who considered students quiet demonstrated fewer school problems and better learning attitudes (Li et al., 2010). In the first case, where students and staff lacked the knowledge of cultural values of their Chinese students, the assumption was that they could not be successful due to a gap in verbal assertion compared to their peers (Li et al., 2010). In the second case, knowledge of the students' cultural background in the school community appeared to facilitate the students' positive experiences in school. So, what role can school counselors play in advancing cultural responsiveness to ensure all students can thrive?

School counselors play a vital role in advocating for a culturally responsive school environment. Under the ASCA Ethical Standards, it states school counselors' responsibility to students in regard to supporting school development include:

a Provide culturally responsive instruction and appraisal and advisement to students.
b Respect students' and families' values, beliefs, and cultural background, as well as students' sexual orientation, gender identity, and gender expression, and exercise great care to avoid imposing personal biases, beliefs, or values rooted in one's religion, culture, or ethnicity.
c Advocate for equitable, anti-oppressive and anti-bias policies and procedures, systems and practices, and provide effective, evidence-based and culturally sustaining interventions to address student needs.

Linking back to its universality, we can insert the opportunity to create art for these students to demonstrate their strengths and ability to communicate through a different medium, all while being able to honor the values of their culture. With the intentional integration of art therapy approaches in a comprehensive school counseling program that reaches all students, the possibilities increase for students to honor their own culture and those of other students. In a study on the relationship between multiculturalism and art, Al-Zadjali (2024) found that participants from various backgrounds engaged and communicated across cultural boundaries thanks to artistic representations. According to the study, cultural festivals and art events allowed for interaction, story exchanges, and gaining knowledge from one another, which promoted respect and admiration for one another. Traditional art forms and indigenous cultural expressions were identified as essential in preserving cultural heritage and promoting a sense of cultural pride among communities. The study also highlighted the need to support and safeguard these art forms to ensure the continuity of cultural identity.

More than Meets the Eye

Creating art provides the opportunity for students to gain something visual and tangible when discussing information about themselves with others. This would be particularly helpful for students whose cultural background considers and interprets eye contact differently than the majority of their peers and school staff. While eye contact is valued and seen as an asset in communication in Western cultures, those from Eastern cultures may believe eye contact to be rude and aggressive (Akechi et al., 2013). This could make sharing and communicating difficult for students if verbal means was the only option. Creating art can be used to share oneself through another medium that does not require eye contact. The student may feel safer pointing and referencing their art when expressing themselves to others.

School counselors can facilitate multiculturalism by providing art therapy-based directives that prompt students with the opportunities to express who they are through a different vehicle that does not involve speaking nor writing. A simple art directive can allow students to embrace their cultural identity, and explore and showcase other aspects that influence who they are. Let's take a look at how this can be done.

2.7   Art to Affirm Self-Identity, Expression, and Inclusion

As part of the pilot group mentioned in Chapter 1, one of the school counselors identified newcomer students to receive art therapy integrated small group as an intervention to close the gap on academic achievement. All of the students had been in the US for less than two years, having immigrated recently from another country, and participating in a small group was a means to ease the transition not only to a new school, but an entirely new life and way of being. Up to this point the process had not been easy, as several factors impacted their ability to progress in school. Though they were eligible to receive ELL services throughout the school day, there had not been a consistent certified ELL Teacher to provide this support for the second school year in a row. On top of that, there were barely any full-time teachers or other staff members who spoke the students' native language to help with translation. Finally, these factors may have caused their inconsistent attendance to school.

The ASCA Ethical Standards, as it relates to group work, is to ensure "equitable access to participation in groups, including alleviating physical, language and other obstacles"(ASCA, 2022, pp 4). Through the advocacy of this school counselor, they were able to have one of the few staff members, a teacher's assistant who was fluent in Spanish, to help translate during the sessions. Also considering the universality of art, facilitating art therapy approaches with the students provided for "culturally sustaining small group services based on individual student, school, and community needs; student data; a referral process; and/or other relevant data"(ASCA, 2022, pp 4). Though they had a translator, the art created during the group sessions further enhanced the connection between the school counselor and the small group of students that didn't rely only on verbal or written means.

In one small group session, students were given the art directive to create self-identity flags. Through this directive, students created flags based on prompts to explore further who they are and how this can be represented in their flags (See Table 2.1). The students were then encouraged to use their answers to create drawings and symbols they wanted to include in their flags. As a result,

Table 2.1 Prompts to facilitate ideas for self-identity flags

Self-Identity Flag Prompts

What does your name mean? What does your name mean to you?
What is your cultural background?
What are your favorite colors?
What do you value? (i.e., kindness, fairness, respect)
What are your hobbies, talents, or interests?
What are three things you like about yourself?
What brings you joy?

Figure 2.2 Examples of self-identity flags created by students to represent who they are (a–d).

they were able to share their flags with others, garnering encouragement to be proud of something that represented themselves.

Once the students created their flags, they had a chance to reflect and write in their native language about the experience of making their identity flags. They were able to share with the group their reflections, enhancing their abilities to communicate and connect with one another. This fostered an understanding of one another, empathy, and appreciation for their diversity as well as their commonalities. This set up a path for them to see themselves in others, lessening any feelings of isolation. You can see some examples of these flags in Figure 2.2.

Integrating an art therapy-based directive, such as self-identity flags, provides an opportunity for students to create extensions of themselves that they can take pride in. Affirming the art as a school counselor and encouraging the same among the students themselves helps to establish a safe, equitable, affirming school environment in which all members are respected and feel included (American School Counselor Association, 2021). With the consent of the students, their artwork can be displayed in common areas, increasing the likelihood of students' sense of belonging in school. See Lesson 2.1 on creating self-identity flags in the Appendix.

2.8 Trauma: A Matter of Equity

If we take a step back and reflect on trauma amongst youth across the US, we will find that the prevalence of trauma is higher than many might expect. More than two-thirds of children reported at least one traumatic event by age 16. Being aware of the statistics and how it impacts youth and their learning in school is important in order to identify evidence-based interventions appropriate to address trauma. Potentially traumatic events include:

Psychological, physical, or sexual abuse; community or school violence; witnessing or experiencing domestic violence; national disasters or terrorist; commercial sexual exploitation; sudden or violent loss of a loved one; refugee or war experiences; military family-related stressors (e.g., deployment, parental loss or injury); physical or sexual assault; neglect; or serious accidents or life-threatening illness (Substance Abuse and Mental Health Services Administration, n.d.).

Another important factor to consider is the data on trauma when it comes to marginalized populations, which the ASCA Ethical Standards include as critical to supporting student growth and success in school.

> People who are a part of historically oppressed groups — whether due to race, immigration status, income level, gender identity, sexual orientation, zip code, or other factors — are more likely to experience trauma as a result of that oppression. Moreover, these factors "intersect," compounding the impact of trauma as experiences of discrimination and oppression increase. This is why trauma is fundamentally an issue of equity.
>
> (Chicago Public Schools, 2021, p. 10)

School counselors must understand the impact of Adverse Childhood Experiences (ACEs) on students' academic achievement and social/emotional development (American School Counselor Association, n.d.). Data from the 2016 National Survey of Children's Health (NSCH) as cited in Sacks and Murphey (2018) describe the prevalence of one or more ACEs among children in the US from birth through age 17, as reported by a parent or guardian. With regards to marginalized populations, the study included examining the prevalence differences by race/ethnicity. Nationally, 61% of Black non-Hispanic children and 51% of Hispanic children have experienced at least one ACE, compared with 40% of White non-Hispanic children and only 23% of Asian non-Hispanic children. In another study highlighting the impact of trauma on LGBTQ+ youth found that those who reported high levels of trauma symptoms had three times greater odds of attempting suicide in the past year compared to those with no trauma symptoms and low or moderate trauma symptoms (Johns et al., 2022).

To expect a level of success with the same resources, or even less than those provided to other students who do not possess these traumatic experiences, leaves these students at another disadvantage. A trauma-informed approach to a school counselor's work includes acknowledging this disparity, including the history behind it. In Chicago, for example, there is a history of redlining that occurred during the Great Migration of Black people from the South in the 1930s that placed them with significantly less opportunities than White people, in particular investment in properties (Serrato et al., n.d.). Living in a redlined neighborhood meant there were significantly more Black people in these neighborhoods, which led to less loans granted from banks to purchase homes in these areas, as well as reduced access to healthy food, health care, and more. Compared to schools located in non-redlined neighborhoods of Chicago, you can still see significantly less mental health resources for students residing where red-lining was prominent. To this day, the harmful and enduring effects of redlining continue to impact Black students' graduation and college enrollment rates. This indicates the importance of being aware of how trauma impacts learning.

Unaddressed trauma can show up in negative behaviors in school that disrupt a student's ability to learn, and often a student may not know that this is what is happening. What neuropsychologists have found is that traumatic experiences actually can alter children's brains. In times of great stress or trauma, the brain activates its deeply instinctive "fight, flight, or freeze" responses while dialing down the areas of the brain where learning, especially around language, takes place. When this happens repeatedly, especially in children under age 5, the brain is fundamentally changed (Flannery, 2016). It adapts for survival under the worst conditions (Flannery, 2016). During a traumatic experience, the Broca's area, or speech center located on the left side of the brain, shuts down during trauma (Dogan & BVSc, 2024). As a result, verbalizing trauma is difficult, making talk therapy by itself insufficient to heal post-traumatic stress disorder (PTSD) or secondary traumatic stress disorder (STSD) (Dogan & BVSc, 2024). Given the impact of trauma on the brain, student learning, and speech, how can school counselors use this information to inform their practice?

2.9 Art Therapy Integration as a Trauma-Informed Approach

Juliet King, an art therapist, gave a compelling presentation to emphasize how the brain works when it comes to memories, trauma, and distress (Cultural Programs of the National Academy of Sciences [CPNAS], 2018). King asked the audience to close their eyes and think of water. When asked, a few participants shared what came up for them. One participant shared that they envisioned a waterfall, another an ocean, to which King pointed out that it is rare that a person would envision the spelled-out word "w-a-t-e-r" in their mind. King continues to say that if we understand that science says that our brain holds memories in images, and we know that trauma is held in the part of the brain that we do not have easy verbal access to, we can understand how difficult it is to talk about something upsetting (CPNAS, 2018). Creating art can be used as a medium to discover the need to address the trauma, as it is held in images in the brain rather than in words.

Art therapy may offer an alternative and suitable treatment because the nonverbal and experiential character of art therapy appears to be an appropriate approach to the often wordless and visual nature of traumatic memories (Schouten et al., 2018). School counselors can introduce art as a way for students to gain more information on what is happening to them, for example, the effects of trauma and how that impacts their behavior. The student art provides deeper insight and knowledge, which can then lead to positive ways of coping and responsible decision-making. "Competency development is key to building resilience in students with ACEs" (Rawson, 2021 p. 109). To demonstrate this further, let's take a look at how art therapy approaches can help school counselors provide trauma-informed practices that support competency development.

Referring back to our newcomer students from the pilot program, many of them were refugees due to having to flee their country for safety and survival, and these pre-migration experiences still resonated with them. With simple, art-therapy-based directives through school counseling services, they were able to share these experiences, which led to a path of connection and healing.

During a small group session, students were given an opportunity to experiment with clay – flattening, rolling, twisting, attaching and re-attaching, and exploring all the possibilities the medium can do. They were then asked to create an animal that they'd like to be for a day. The directive intended to explore the strengths and challenges of each animal, and what each one needs to thrive, as described by the student who created it. In one session, a student created a snake, which they described as an animal they saw on their journey to coming to the US. This immediately sparked interest among the other group members, as it led them to commenting on what animals they saw on their journeys. They continued to share their experiences while working on their animals. It was during this session that cohesiveness began, and the school counselor had the opportunity to acknowledge them for not only their ability to communicate and share with one another, but sharing vulnerable information about their long journeys to their new homes, the dangers that were posed, and the continued challenges they were going through adjusting to their new environment. Though simple in nature, highlighting for the students their resilience can help them to see that they are strong, contributing to a sense of confidence in their abilities. You can refer to Lesson 2.2 "Animal for a Day" in the Appendix for entire lesson.

2.10 Trauma-Informed, Art-Therapy Integrated, Crisis Response

When I have had students referred to me for having thoughts of hurting themselves, or suicidal ideation, they were often even more scared due to how their parents, teachers, or peers would take the news, or fear that they were going to be hospitalized. It is a stressful time for a young person, and given the prevalence of ACEs among youth, more likely than not, traumatic experiences in their past are contributing even more to the level of distress. Leaning on neuroscience research from Chapter 1, the calming effects of art-making can be beneficial for a student during this time. Even without a discussion of the art, I've found students to naturally de-escalate and come to be in a less anxious state than when they first came in.

If a student is experiencing a strong and overwhelming emotion, they can depict it through their art, allowing for it to be seen outside of themselves, creating an emotional distance and sense of safety in order to process. Often there is a long wait time for their parents and a crisis worker to arrive, and the student would wait with me for several hours. With art materials easily accessible, students can create as a means to stay calm and to have an outlet for their overwhelming emotions as they wait. Sometimes I'd show them different techniques they can learn with a medium like oil pastels, which helps to keep them in the present and focused on their art. With their art piece, I was able to acknowledge their emotions while also sharing recognition of their ability to focus and be calm during a challenging time. An advantage of the art during a distressing time is that the student can visualize themselves regulating their overwhelming emotions. Figure 2.3 showcases a student's

Figure 2.3 A student's drawing of herself taking deep breaths.

drawing of herself as she takes deep breaths in, which she described were the blue marks on her drawing, and taking deep breaths out, as indicated by the pink marks.

2.11 Conclusion

When students have a visual of themselves coping effectively, it strengthens their belief that they can manage strong emotions that come with stressful events. Integrating art therapy approaches in school counseling practices addresses a significant part of the ASCA Ethical Student Standards when it comes to supporting student development through an equity lens. The use of art by school counselors provides a means for students to embrace who they are, connect with others, instill a sense of belonging at school, and increase their self-confidence, as well as heal, no matter what their background and experiences. This transformative experience through art provides a clearer vision of the future they want to create for themselves.

Now that we've taken a look at how integrating art therapy approaches covers the school counselor's Ethical Standards defined by ASCA, let's take a look at how these approaches help students meet the ASCA Student Standards in Chapter 3.

References

Akechi, H., Senju, A., Uibo, H., Kikuchi, Y., Hasegawa, T., & Hietanen, J. K. (2013). Attention to eye contact in the West and East: Autonomic responses and evaluative ratings. *PLoS One, 8*(3), e59312. https://doi.org/10.1371/journal.pone.0059312

Al-Zadjali, Z. (2024). The significance of art in revealing a culture's identity and multiculturalism. *Open Journal of Social Sciences, 12*(1), 232–250. https://doi.org/10.4236/jss.2024.121015

American School Counselor Association. (n.d.). *The School Counselor and Trauma-Informed Practice*. schoolcounselor.org. Retrieved February 27, 2025, from https://www.schoolcounselor.org/Standards-Positions/Position-Statements/ASCA-Position-Statements/The-School-Counselor-and-Trauma-Informed-Practice#:~:text=ASCA%20Position,students%20who%20have%20experienced%20trauma.

American School Counselor Association. (2021). *The School Counselor and Cultural Diversity*. https://www.schoolcounselor.org/Standards-Positions/Position-Statements/ASCA-Position-Statements/The-School-Counselor-and-Cultural-Diversity#:~:text=School%20counselors%20can%20provide%20culturally,students%20in%20diverse%20cultural%20groups

American School Counselor Association. (2022). *ASCA Ethical Standards for School Counselors*. https://www.schoolcounselor.org/getmedia/44f30280-ffe8-4b41-9ad8-f15909c3d164/EthicalStandards.pdf

Cultural Programs of the National Academy of Sciences [CPNAS]. (2018, October 3). *Juliet King: Art Therapy and Neuroscience: A Revitalized Synthesis* [Video]. YouTube. https://youtu.be/TeD3xyFSdoI?si=j6_D81q_ihNK-XgI

Dogan, Hilal & BVSc, CCTP. (2024, April 19). This is your brain on trauma. *DVM 360*. https://www.dvm360.com/view/your-brain-trauma

Edelman, M. W. (2021, June 22). Marian Wright Edelman: Connecting Through Children's Books. *The Philadelphia Tribune*. https://www.phillytrib.com/commentary/marian-wright-edelman-connecting-through-children-s-books/article_fe787ed5-303e-568b-ad09-75b17a523188.html

Flannery, M. E. (2016, May 17). *How Trauma is Changing Children's Brains | NEA*. https://www.nea.org/nea-today/all-news-articles/how-trauma-changing-childrens-brains#:~:text=What%20neuropsychologists%20have%20found%20is,survival%20under%20the%20worst%20conditions.

Johns, E. Al., Meyers, Nadal, E. Al., Almeida, E. Al., Roberts, E. Al., & Williams, E. Al. (2022). *Trauma and suicide risk among LGBTQ youth*. https://www.thetrevorproject.org/wp-content/uploads/2022/07/July-Brief-Trauma-Among-LGBTQ-Youth.pdf

Keane, C. (2017, May 11). *An expert on school-based art therapy explains how art therapy helps children make sense of the insensible*. American Art Therapy Association. https://arttherapy.org/art-therapy-helps-children-make-sense-of-the-insensible/

Li, J., Yamamoto, Y., Luo, L., Batchelor, A. K., & Bresnahan, R. M. (2010). Why attend school? Chinese immigrant and European American preschoolers' views and outcomes. *Developmental Psychology, 46*(6), 1637–1650. https://doi.org/10.1037/a0019926

National Center for Education Statistics. (2020, September). *Race and Ethnicity of Public School Teachers and Their Students*. Retrieved February 27, 2025, from https://nces.ed.gov/pubs2020/2020103/index.asp

Rawson, S. (2021). *Applying trauma-sensitive practices in school counseling*. Routledge.

Sacks, V., & Murphey, D. (2018). The prevalence of adverse childhood experiences, nationally, by state, and by race or ethnicity. In ChildTrends. https://www.childtrends.org/publications/prevalence-adverse-childhood-experiences-nationally-state-race-ethnicity

Schouten, K. A., Van Hooren, S., Knipscheer, J. W., Kleber, R. J., & Hutschemaekers, G. J. (2018). Trauma-focused art therapy in the treatment of Posttraumatic stress disorder: A pilot study. *Journal of Trauma & Dissociation, 20*(1), 114–130. https://doi.org/10.1080/15299732.2018.1502712

Serrato, J., Sier, P., & Runes, C. (n.d.). *Mapping Chicago's racial segregation*. WTTW.

Srinivasan, M. (2019). *SEL every day: Integrating social and emotional learning with instruction in secondary classrooms (SEL Solutions Series)*. National Geographic Books.

Zirkel, S. (2002). Is there a place for me? role models and academic identity among white students and students of color. *Teachers College Record the Voice of Scholarship in Education, 104*(2), 357–376. https://doi.org/10.1177/016146810210400206

Chapter 3

Art Therapy Approaches and School Counseling
Alignment with ASCA Student Standards

3.1 Art Therapy Approaches and the ASCA Student Standards

In Chapter 2, we covered how integrating art therapy into school counseling approaches can help school counselors address key ethical standards, ensuring equitable, quality, and accessible education for all. This chapter will focus on how art therapy through school counseling services can also help students to learn and achieve the American School Counselor Association (ASCA) student standards. These core standards are qualities that students should acquire throughout their education and development to support and encourage their success in school, college, career, and general adult life (American School Counselor Association, 2021). You can see these core standards in Figure 3.1.

The ASCA Student Standards are largely based on a review of research titled "Teaching Adolescents to Become Learners," conducted by the University of Chicago Consortium on Chicago School Research (Farrington et al., 2012). This review is a compilation of evidence that shows that non-cognitive factors, such as positive mindsets, social skills, and academic perseverance, are essential to children's learning and development at all ages and grade levels (Farrington et al., 2012). Furthermore, these factors are not defined as fixed traits that students either possess or lack, but as characteristics that can be learned (Farrington et al., 2012).

What makes these standards "non-cognitive" is that they are not measured through quizzes, exams, or tests in the way academic skills and content knowledge are assessed. The mindsets encompass what students should believe, or attitudes they need to carry toward school to ensure lifelong success. The standards also include behaviors we want students to demonstrate, such as learning strategies, self-management skills, and social skills that are connected to academic achievement (ASCA, 2021). School counselors can help students achieve

DOI: 10.4324/9781003430940-5

**ASCA Student Standards: Mindsets & Behaviors for Student Success
K-12 College-, Career- and Life-Readiness Standards for Every Student**

Each of the following standards can be applied to the academic, career and social/emotional domains.

Category 1: Mindset Standards
School counselors encourage the following mindsets for all students.

M 1. Belief in development of whole self, including a healthy balance of mental, social/emotional and physical well-being
M 2. Sense of acceptance, respect, support and inclusion for self and others in the school environment
M 3. Positive attitude toward work and learning
M 4. Self-confidence in ability to succeed
M 5. Belief in using abilities to their fullest to achieve high-quality results and outcomes
M 6. Understanding that postsecondary education and lifelong learning are necessary for long-term success

Category 2: Behavior Standards
School counselors provide culturally sustaining instruction, appraisal and advisement, and counseling to help all students demonstrate:

Learning Strategies		Self-Management Skills		Social Skills	
B-LS 1.	Critical thinking skills to make informed decisions	**B-SMS 1.**	Responsibility for self and actions	**B-SS 1.**	Effective oral and written communication skills and listening skills
B-LS 2.	Creative approach to learning, tasks and problem solving	**B-SMS 2.**	Self-discipline and self-control	**B-SS 2.**	Positive, respectful and supportive relationships with students who are similar to and different from them
B-LS 3.	Time-management, organizational and study skills	**B-SMS 3.**	Independent work	**B-SS 3.**	Positive relationships with adults to support success
B-LS 4.	Self-motivation and self-direction for learning	**B-SMS 4.**	Delayed gratification for long-term rewards	**B-SS 4.**	Empathy
B-LS 5.	Media and technology skills to enhance learning	**B-SMS 5.**	Perseverance to achieve long- and short-term goals	**B-SS 5.**	Ethical decision-making and social responsibility
B-LS 6.	High-quality standards for tasks and activities	**B-SMS 6.**	Ability to identify and overcome barriers	**B-SS 6.**	Effective collaboration and cooperation skills
B-LS 7.	Long- and short-term academic, career and social/emotional goals	**B-SMS 7.**	Effective coping skills	**B-SS 7.**	Leadership and teamwork skills to work effectively in diverse groups
B-LS 8	Engagement in challenging coursework	**B-SMS 8.**	Balance of school, home and community activities	**B-SS 8.**	Advocacy skills for self and others and ability to assert self, when necessary
B-LS 9.	Decision-making informed by gathering evidence, getting others' perspectives and recognizing personal bias	**B-SMS 9.**	Personal safety skills	**B-SS 9.**	Social maturity and behaviors appropriate to the situation and environment
B-LS 10.	Participation in enrichment and extracurricular activities	**B-SMS 10.**	Ability to manage transitions and adapt to change	**B-SS 10.**	Cultural awareness, sensitivity and responsiveness

Figure 3.1 The ASCA Student Standards: Mindsets and behaviors for student success (American School Counselor Association, 2021).

these skills by supporting healthy development and success in school and how this relates to their future goals. For example:

- They can teach students the importance of arriving to school on time.
- They can emphasize the importance of organizing assignments and turning them in by the due date.
- They can support students as they persevere through challenges, such as difficult math problems that take time to understand and practice to solve.

- They can help them set goals and identify actions steps to achieve them,.
- They can demonstrate empathy and serve as a role model for other students.
- They can encourage respectful behavior toward themselves and others, making school an inclusive place.

And the list goes on to address the non-cognitive factors for student success.

It may be useful to visualize the ASCA standards applied across three broad domains: academic, social-emotional, and career. When students are provided equal access to learning the skills in all three domains, they are better positioned for graduation and long-term success (see Figure 3.2). More attention spent on one domain at the expense of the others limits students' access to comprehensive learning and developing the non-cognitive traits. So how can these standards be taught to an entire student body?

School counselors can balance and deliver these standards across the three domains using the Multi-Tiered, Multi-Domain System of Support (MTMDSS) (Hatching Results, 2024). The MTMDSS framework organizes the program of school counseling program services into three levels of tiered support: Tier 1

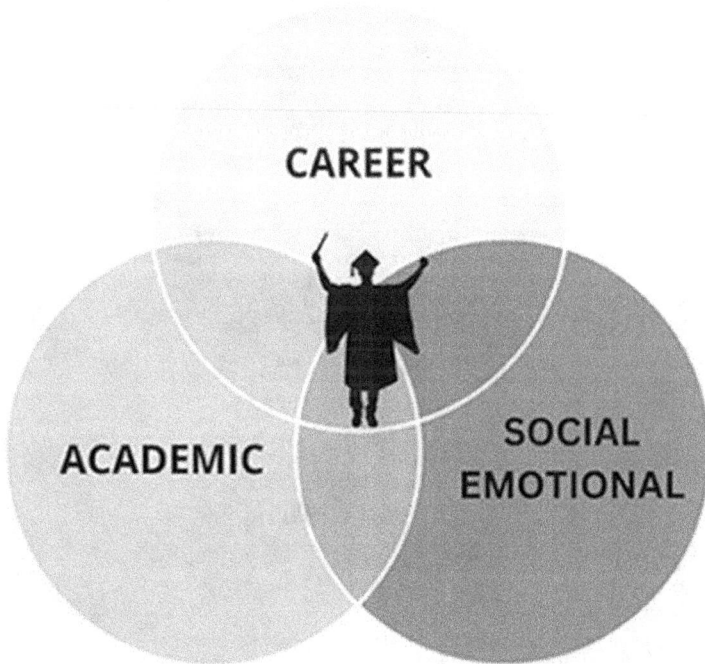

Figure 3.2 The ASCA Student Standards can be applied to three broad domains: academic, social-emotional, and career.

universal supports, Tier 2 targeted supports, and Tier 3 intensified supports. These varying levels of services ensure that all students have access to learning the ASCA Student Standards in all three domains of school counseling: academic, college and career, and social/emotional. You can see this in Figure 3.3.

Now that we've reviewed the ASCA Student Standards, and how school counselors provide access to learning these skills, we will explore how art therapy approaches can be integrated into the delivery of school counseling services so that all students have access to developing these competencies critical to success. Tier I, universal programming that reaches all students, such as classroom instruction, and Tier II Services, such as small group and individual counseling, to reach a fewer students, will be discussed.

So, how do art therapy approaches fit into this structure of school counseling services and address the ASCA student standards? First, integrating art therapy approaches into counseling sessions with students helps make learning the standards engaging. Creating art takes advantage of the students' natural instinct to be creative and expressive, and allows them to take risks through their own art. And how can we know? Although it may not be evident in their final exams, student learning of the mindsets and behaviors can be seen visually through their art. A student witnessing their personal growth and learning of critical skills through their artwork is meaningful and profound because it is connected to something they have made.

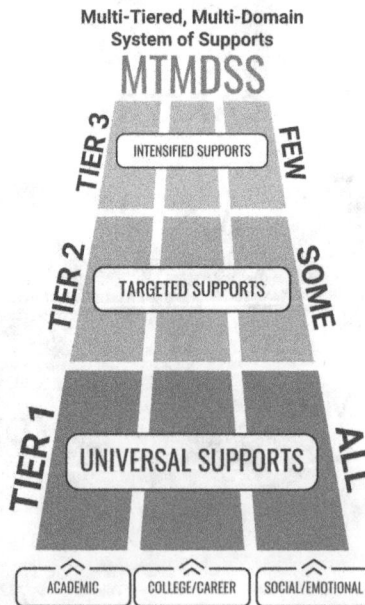

Multi-Tiered, Multi-Domain
System of Supports
MTMDSS

TIER 3   INTENSIFIED SUPPORTS   FEW

TIER 2   TARGETED SUPPORTS   SOME

TIER 1   UNIVERSAL SUPPORTS   ALL

ACADEMIC   COLLEGE/CAREER   SOCIAL/EMOTIONAL

Figure 3.3 Multi-tiered, multi-domain system of supports (MTMDSS) (Hatching Results, 2024).

In this chapter, we will explore through several case studies how integrating art therapy approaches through the tiered levels of counseling services helped students learn the ASCA Student Standards in addressing the three domains, supporting their development and success inside and outside of school.

3.2   Tier I: Classroom Instruction

Student Art and the Academic Domain

It was the beginning of a new school year, and I started co-teaching lessons to students in eighth grade. These lessons were from a new curriculum that primarily focused on the career domain, with integrated mindsets and behaviors from the academic and social-emotional learning (SEL). domains. For example, while some of the lessons focused specifically on exploring different careers, others focused on the skills that support academic achievement as a means to prepare students for their chosen careers. These academic lessons included students learning how their grades in each subject were calculated, how to compute their grade point average, and how to organize their work. And others included SEL skills, teaching students how to ask for help when struggling academically, and how to work effectively with classmates on a group project.

As I followed each lesson in the curriculum, I realized I was providing more of what they would do in other academic classes, such as worksheets, presentations, and "do-nows," or questions that involved writing down their comprehension of a particular topic. I'm not saying that any of these teaching methods are better or worse than others, but I recognized that it only allowed for participation through verbal and written means. Those who struggled with writing in general, or those who weren't as confident in raising their hands to answer questions, were unable to demonstrate their learning. At that time, I knew I wanted to break up the monotony, in order to increase overall engagement in the lessons and providing a different way for the students to learn and demonstrate their understanding. For the next lesson, I decided to steer in a different direction so that students had the opportunity to be creative and envision the future they wanted for themselves. For this particular lesson (See Lesson 3.1 in the Appendix), I identified Mindset 4, "Self-confidence in their ability to succeed, along with self-motivation and self-direction for learning," or Behavior Learning Strategy (BLS-4). These standards were chosen for two reasons: (1) eighth grade is a critical year for students as it is the year before making a significant transition to high school and; (2) it was in response to teachers and staff commenting on how the students that year seemed apathetic towards school compared to previous years. We saw several students coming in late, lacking attention and focus in the classroom, and overall appearing unmotivated. I'd often hear students in the hallway or in class say, "I can't wait to get out of this school!"

According to research conducted by the University of Chicago Consortium on Chicago School Research, indicators for high school and college success are strongly connected to eighth-grade grades and attendance (Allensworth et al., 2014). One key finding included in the research report is that eighth-grade students with GPAs of at least 3.0 have a moderate chance of earning a 3.0 GPA in high school, a benchmark for being considered "college-bound." Considering these indicators for high school and college success, I wanted eighth-grade students to be aware of this data to help them make informed decisions. In the lesson, I presented graphs to provide a visual representation of the research on eighth-grade GPA and attendance as two key indicators that predicted the likelihood of being on track to high school graduation as a ninth-grade student (Allensworth et al., 2014). I asked the students to study the graphs and, when ready, volunteer to name what factors were shown to contribute to being successful in high school. The students recognized that their performance in their current year as an eighth-grade student impacted their future in high school. Upon learning this information, several students appeared shocked. I then reminded students that having this information can be a benefit to help them to make decisions and determine how they want their eighth-grade year to go. From there, they can take the action steps needed to ultimately reach their goals.

In order to help the students create their plans for eighth grade, I asked the class how many of them would like to graduate in June and be on a path to graduation in high school and then on to college and career. All the students raised their hands. I acknowledged their collective goal and let them know I would help them create a plan with actionable steps to get them there. Next, I asked them to draw what they would look like on Graduation Day. The students had colored pencils, markers, and I provided a sheet of 11" × 17" paper that had a pre-drawn silhouette outline of a student in a graduation cap and gown. I asked them to envision what that day would look like, who would be there, what they would be feeling and thinking, and any other factors they felt would be important to include in their Graduation Day drawings. See Figure 3.4 of a student's vision of their graduation day.

The beauty of art is that it can show a side of students that is often hidden, breaking any misconceptions of their attitudes toward school or their future. For example, if a student comes in late every day, it is assumed that they just don't care enough about being in school; or if they don't turn in their assignments they are lazy and unmotivated; or that teenagers are being teenagers and they need to be serious if they want to graduate. In contrast to this perception, the completed "Graduation Day" drawings illustrated common themes, such as a sense of hope, feelings of happiness and pride, a sense of accomplishment, embracing the future, identifying their support system, and the academic goals set for the current year. When it may appear that students don't care about school, or even when they state that they don't, most likely it's quite the contrary.

Figure 3.4 A student drawing of their goals for the school year, eighth-grade graduation day, and their support system.

Seeing Is Believing...and Motivating

An advantage of creating art as part of the lesson is that it can be used to instill confidence. As the goal was to teach Mindset 4, "Self-confidence in their ability to succeed," students were reminded that they completed something that represents their success. It can help them build their confidence as the art serves as evidence that they can complete a task at hand. Being able to create something strengthens their attachment to it, and their art can serve as visual motivation to take action toward a goal they would like to achieve – graduating from eighth grade and having a successful start in high school. Students were encouraged to use their pictures to decide what steps they would need to take to ensure their daily efforts aligned with their goals. They were asked to think about any foreseen challenges on the way to reaching their goal of graduation. If they had trouble getting to school on time, they were asked what action steps could be taken on their part to create change? Could they prepare their backpacks and clothes the night before? Leave 10 minutes earlier than usual? If they had difficulty in math, what resources were available to help them? Could they take advantage of their teacher's offer for help before school or during lunch? Are their tutoring services available after school? Using the art to serve as their end goal, they can identify resources and action steps to get there. Integrating the benefits of an art therapy approach in classroom instruction that year helped students learn the critical ASCA Standards that laid the foundation for their last year in middle school and helped them be prepared for high school.

Student Art and the Career Domain

One of the most rewarding aspects that I have found in being a school counselor is when a student has that "a-ha" moment – when they realize that they can find a career that matches their interests, hobbies, talents, values, and working style, all while getting paid. Mindset 6 of the ASCA Student Standards is the understanding that postsecondary education and lifelong learning are necessary for long-term career success. School counselors introduce the world of work and facilitate student exploration of all career possibilities.

Early adolescence is a pivotal time in a student's life to start career exploration, as this is when they begin to seek out who they are and what purpose they have in the world. Erik Erikson's (1958, 1963) as cited in McLeod (2024) Humanistic Theory of psychosocial development called this the "identity vs confusion" stage, which occurs between 12 and 18 years old. During this period, adolescents explore possibilities and begin to form their own identities based on the outcome of their explorations. Failure to establish a sense of identity within society ("I don't know what I want to be when I grow up") can lead to role confusion (Erikson, 1958/1963 as cited in McLeod, 2024). School counselors can help guide students to successful completion of this stage by helping them gain a sense of self, who they want to be, and be sure of their place in society.

Since the students found drawing their future self-portraits graduating from eighth grade to be both impactful and academically motivating, I integrated this art therapy approach when it came to learning more about themselves and how it would relate to a career. Several lessons in the career exploration unit consisted of interest inventories, introduction of career clusters, and pathways to different careers. Students also researched careers that matched their talents, interests, hobbies, personality traits, and preferences in work environments. They reviewed results from interest inventories and career cluster surveys, and researched career outlooks, salaries, required training, and education in different careers. From there, they narrowed their career interests to a "Top 3."

To complement the learning in the career domain, in the next lesson, I asked students to visualize what having a dream career looked like to them. If they hadn't chosen a specific career at that point, or they had an interest in several different ones, I asked them to think about how they would want to feel in their dream career. Happy, confident, using their special interests and talents? What would their work setting look like? Do they like working with a team of people? Do they want to serve in a leadership role? I asked them to draw it all out.

Soon after, I observed that all students on this day, more than any other day, started on the task assigned immediately. From those who typically needed redirection to the task, to those who often appeared disinterested in class, what they all had in common was an eagerness to start right away. They grabbed laptops to look for images related to their dream careers, along with all of their art materials, such as markers, colored pencils, and multi-media paper, and immediately started researching and drawing out their careers. See Figure 3.5 for student "Dream Career" drawings.

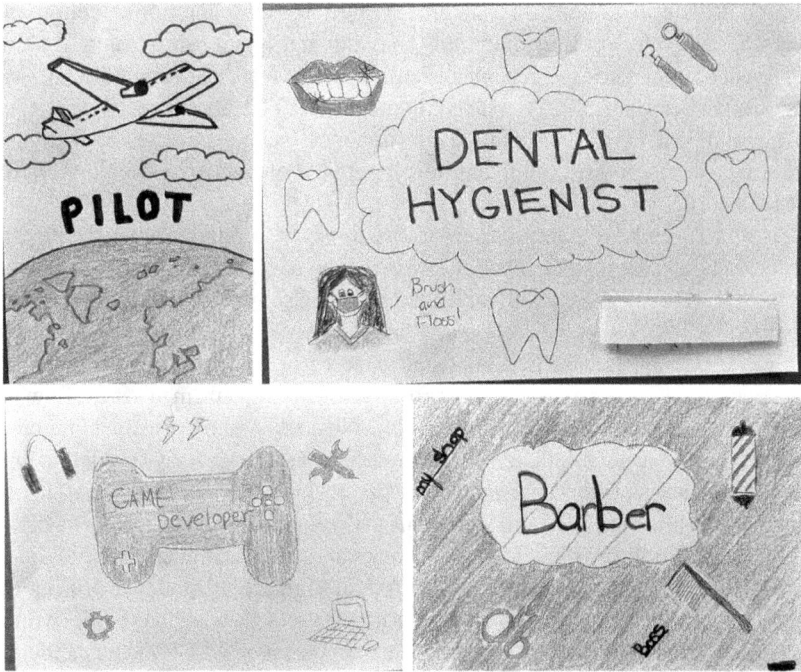

Figures 3.5 Students express their dream careers through art (a–d).

After all of the students created their art representing their dream career, I led a discussion with the students to help them understand that it is never too early to start thinking about their future. In the following lessons, I used their Dream Career Drawings to connect what they do now in school, or their short-term goals, can impact their future and help them obtain their long-term goals, or B-SMS 5 of the ASCA Student Standards. The drawings served as a tool for appraisal, as I was able to use them when advising the students on the pathway to take to their dream career. Using their drawing as a visual reference, students were able to map out their pathways and learn what education and training were needed to achieve their goals. If a student wanted to become a chef, they learned that it required graduating from high school and going on to culinary school. If a student wanted to become a lawyer, they learned that they needed to obtain an undergraduate degree and then go on to law school.

Once the drawings were completed, the Dream Career Drawings were displayed in the hallway to serve as inspiration not only for the eighth grade students, but for the younger students in the building, emphasizing a school culture of college and career success.

Student Art and the Social-Emotional Learning (SEL) Domain

The third domain that the ASCA Student Standards address is SEL. For school counselors, this translates into teaching the SEL-related non-cognitive factors that contribute to lifelong success, including managing emotions, feeling and showing empathy, establishing and maintaining relationships, and making responsible and caring decisions (Collaborative for Academic, Social, and Emotional Learning, 2023). SEL skills as part of education have been linked to positive outcomes in academic performance, school climate, and graduation rates, among other significant developmental outcomes. (Collaborative for Academic, Social, and Emotional Learning, 2025)

The SEL needs of students came to the forefront during the COVID-19 pandemic. School communities across the district expressed concern about the student's emotional well-being, especially given the sudden disruption to their daily routines. For many students, school had been the only consistent setting in their lives before the pandemic. In response to school staff concerns, I was fortunate to find digital resources that allowed students to be exposed to art, allowing them to benefit from the healing effects of creating art. I planned virtual lessons to emphasize the importance of attending to mental health, and the art created and shared in the virtual world with their classmates and teachers inspired a sense of hope during this period of uncertainty. It also provided an alternative means to communicate and connect with others in the class other than writing in the chat box or unmuting their microphone to speak.

One virtual lesson I hosted was with senior high school students. During the lesson, the students expressed feeling stressed about their school work, worrying about friends and family, and overall disappointment with how the pandemic had drastically changed their final years in high school. I acknowledged that their awareness of how difficult it was to transition to remote learning and having to adapt to change so quickly was a step toward making sure they could persevere through the challenges.

I then asked the students to choose a word from a list of inspirational words that were in the slide presentation provided to them. They were also able to choose a word or phrase not on the list as long as they found it inspirational. The students were provided an online drawing tool where they could type their inspirational word or phrase anywhere on their virtual paper, and then use the drawing and painting tools available on the platform to create art around the words. I played instrumental lo-fi music as they created independently. Once they completed their digital art, students were able to share their art on screen with the class if they felt comfortable. See Figure 3.6 for examples of student drawings created and shared virtually.

Figure 3.6 During the COVID-19 pandemic lockdown, students created inspirational art online (a and b).

I led the discussion and shared how each drawing was unique, and at the same time had common themes through choices of color, designs, and symbols. When asked what they thought about the lesson, students stated it helped them feel calm and relaxed. I recommended that they continue this during their own time, especially when they felt stressed, and that they could do it online on a presentation deck, or simply with a piece of paper and pencil or pen. As long as they find this to be a means to cope effectively (B-SMS 7), they can create art.

The effects of the pandemic lasted after the return to school, and the mental health of students remained at the forefront of the school community's concerns. As part of Mental Health Awareness Week, I provided a lesson to high school seniors. See Lesson 3.2 in the Appendix. At the time of the lesson, the students were close to the end of the school year and at a time where they were juggling multiple tasks to complete in order to graduate. They were preparing to take Advanced Placement exams, completing end-of-semester assignments, projects, final exams, and planning for college and work. The beginning of the lesson focused on the importance of persevering to achieve their goals, whether long or short-term, during stressful times. The students shared what helped them to cope positively with stress, whether that was talking to a friend, taking a walk or running, or playing sports. Following this discussion, I introduced research to the students on the destressing qualities of creating art. The students learned that no matter their skills or abilities, being part of the process of creating art can be beneficial.

As we were back in person, students could choose one sticker among a selection of stickers with inspirational phrases, place it on their paper, and create around it in any way they wanted to. For the remainder of the class period, students focused on their art. Throughout this time, many appeared calm and focused while they created, which is what they shared during the discussion that followed. Students were reminded that they can do art anywhere, translating this to other settings as appropriate and using it as a means to cope effectively and stay motivated and inspired during stressful times. Whether it be to take a break from studying – reading and writing, or working on complicated math problems – they can stop and freely sketch to step away from the intensity of studying. Before the end of class, students were encouraged to display their inspirational art in a place where they could see it often and be reminded that they can persevere through challenges. You can see examples of these drawings in Figure 3.7.

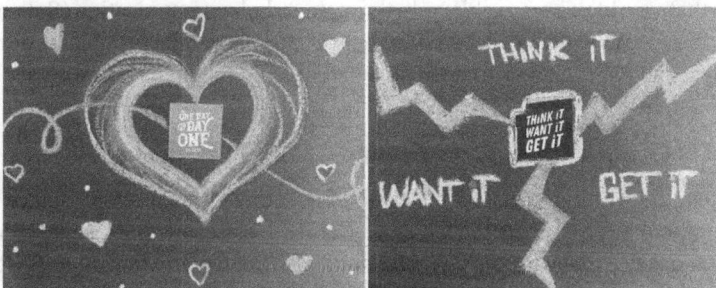

Figure 3.7 Students created inspirational art to motivate them to get through the remainder of the school year (a and b).

3.3   School Counseling Services beyond Classroom Instruction

When students are unable to learn the ASCA Standards at Tier I, i.e. through classroom instruction, school counselors can provide support at a Tier II level in addition to Tier I services. School counselors can review data and identify students with lower grades, a higher number of discipline referrals, or lower attendance than their peers. They can also obtain information from teachers on contributing factors such as the students' behaviors in class, i.e., getting easily frustrated or distracted, or leaving assignments incomplete, not asking for help. This information can help determine what type of Tier II Intervention is needed. There are also times when we, as school counselors and staff, are already aware of what could be impacting students' ability to achieve. For example, students who are going through challenging times such as losing a family member, their parents divorcing, or, as mentioned in Chapter 2, have experienced a significant amount of trauma. These factors can have a serious impact on student well-being, let alone their ability to achieve academically.

Once the root causes of their inability to learn are identified, an appropriate short-term Tier II intervention can be chosen. One such intervention includes having a student work among a smaller group of students compared to the classroom. Being in this setting helps students obtain more attention to their specific needs. Additionally, they may benefit from being with a few others who are experiencing the same challenges. Within this setting, the small group of students can develop supportive relationships amongst each other as they have shared goals (ASCA, 2008). Let's explore how art therapy approaches can support students learning the ASCA standards in a small group setting.

3.4   Art Therapy Approaches in Small Groups

Given the ability of art to form connections and facilitate communication among group members, integrating art therapy in small groups can enhance the experience in the group to learn mindsets and behaviors in a safe way that maximizes the desired outcomes. Whether it's identifying commonalities in individual art or coming together to create one art piece, art in a group forms bonds with others in a way that wouldn't be possible only through verbal communication (Sutherland et al., 2010). What the art does is serve as a safe place to start, a point of reference that can pave the way to open up a verbal dialogue. Let's take a closer look.

Case Study: Fifth Grade Girls' Group

One year, four fifth grade students came to my office often seeking solace from the conflicts ensued throughout the day among classmates, especially during lunch and recess. For these particular students, the tension during their school day impacted them in a significant way, as they all reported that home life was stressful. One commonality they had was that their parents often fought at home, or they had this same experience previously, before their parents divorced or separated. In our first few small group sessions, they admitted to having little interest in school at times and that it was difficult to focus in class. The group members had already started to support each other before joining the group, sharing that at times they would be up late at night talking on the phone as a way to relieve the frustration of their challenging home lives. However, they also expressed being upset with each other at times, whether it be that they "talked behind their back," or called each other out for starting "drama." This then spilled out to the larger spaces in the classroom, and during lunch and recess time, involving other classmates. Upon consulting with their teacher, I learned that she also had concern for this group of girls, especially when they lacked focus and seemed preoccupied, and she was aware that one of them was going through a stressful time dealing with her parents' divorce case.

Animal for a Day: Part I

For these students in small group, I selected Mindset 2 – sense of acceptance, respect, support, and inclusion for self and others in the school environment (American School Counselor Association, 2021) – as the standard to focus on and strengthen. I chose this mindset as I observed the girls to have feelings of sadness and frustration when they were in conflict with each other, and it appeared to have affected their sense of acceptance. After all, their home environments were unstable at the time, and adding in conflict with friends at school could impact their feelings of self-worth. These were two places they spent the most time. The goal for this group was for them to accept themselves and others despite challenges at home or at school, and address any barriers that prevented them from doing so. As they all valued their friendships with each other, the first part of the plan was to help them understand themselves and one another through art, then learn how to communicate with each other in a healthy and positive way.

Based on Mindset 2, and the ability for art to serve as a vehicle to learn new skills, I used the "Animal for a Day" Lesson mentioned in Chapter 2 to help students create an art piece they can connect with, hopefully leading to a discussion of the importance of accepting, respecting, and including oneself and others in the school environment. When I asked them to create their chosen animal with air-dry clay, they all started immediately rolling the clay, flattening it, making limbs, all excitedly sharing what animal they would be. They started forming their animals and, since time allowed, I asked them to create another piece for their animal to help their animal feel comfortable, whether that be food, or a bed, or anything that would make their animals happy.

While their animals were drying, they were given the opportunity to share what animal they chose and why. While they were sharing their animals, I encouraged the group members to ask questions about each other's animals – in particular to the strengths they believed their animals had. For example, the group noticed that one of the animals was a bunny with large ears. One expressed that the ears probably helped them to hear really well, which is good for any sounds in the wild that could mean danger for the bunny. Another member said that the bunny could also be a really good listener, making them a good friend to talk to. The group was also encouraged to share any challenges their animal may have that they wanted the other animals to know about. One student shared that her turtle was very slow due to her short legs and heavy shell. When I asked why it was important for others to know this, she stated that way they won't get mad at her if it takes her longer to get somewhere. When I asked the other members if they would be mad at her for this, they all answered no, explaining that they could be patient. After they all shared about their animals, I shared with them that they all seemed to be accepting of their animals, both strengths and weaknesses. I added that even when animals aren't perfect, it doesn't mean they aren't worthy of having good things in their lives – friends, family, food, safe shelter. I then asked them how they can transfer this mindset toward themselves and to others, even during stressful times. They remained silent as they looked at their animals. I let them know they could think about it until the following week when they were be able to paint their animals. Figure 3.8 is a clay figure created by a group member who expressed wanting to be a bunny for a day.

Animal for a Day: Part II

In the next session, the students were able to paint their animal clay sculptures that had dried since the last session. The learning objective focused on the latter part of Mindset 2, a sense of acceptance, respect, and inclusion of others.

Figure 3.8 A group member created a clay bunny to represent the animal she would like to be for a day.

Referencing their animal sculptures, I asked the group how their animal could help the other animals now that they knew more about each other. This helped to emphasize their skills in being inclusive of one another as well as having empathy for other animals who may have challenges (i.e. being slow, shy, startled easily, quick to react, etc.). Afterward, they were asked about their animals as a collective, and what they believed would make for a safe environment for them all to share and be comfortable. This led to a discussion of the need for trees, shelter, water sources such as ponds, and food that was accessible and inclusive to their specific diets. I used this opportunity to lead the discussion on what made them feel safe and taken care of at school, and how they can make themselves and others feel comfortable in all school settings. Could they ask to speak to one another directly instead of through others if there is a misunderstanding? Can this help to avoid rumors or others being accused of "talking behind their back?" The students were encouraged to choose actions that would help them build healthy interpersonal skills with others.

The following group sessions continued to build on their sense of self-respect and that of others. During the last session of the group, members were invited to create art cards. The objective to create art cards was to have a tangible record of their time in group and to remind them of the lessons learned. The first step was to write their name on the front of their card and to draw around it. Afterward, they passed their card to a group member next to them, whose instructions were to draw symbol or image for that group member's card. This passing and drawing of the cards continued until the art card returned to its original owner. During the final discussion, I pointed out to the students that they seemed to grow in respect of themselves and one another, and that they seemed to communicate with one another in a more positive way. I encouraged them to use their art cards as a visual reminder of how they learned these skills throughout their time together in group. See the Art Card Lesson 3.3 in the Appendix.

3.5   Art Therapy Approaches in Individual Counseling

There are times where students need a higher level of intervention beyond small group to support their learning of the ASCA Student Standards. Individual counseling is appropriate for students when working with others in the classroom environment or in a small group is challenging for them, whether it may be due to a lack in social or cognitive skills, where connecting with others would be difficult. Individual, short-term counseling is a Tier II Intervention that school counselors can provide as a means to provide more individualized attention when teaching the mindsets and behaviors. Integrating art therapy approaches may be a particularly beneficial tool to help students needing this level of support to build their capacity in a safe way to connect, then eventually translate these skills to a small group and classroom settings. These were goals outlined for Olivia and Ethan.

Case Study: Olivia

Olivia was a second grade student who was referred to school counseling due to her behavior. She often yelled back at teachers and other students, was out of her seat, and disrupted others' work. She would sometimes leave the classroom altogether without permission and see herself to my office. Olivia struggled academically, and her grandmother, who was her primary caregiver, added that she did not want to go to school because Olivia believed that no one in her class liked her. When she was in school, she would often say school was "boring" and would state, "I don't care about school anyway." In order to address her academic needs, Olivia received support from a reading interventionist and was sent to the first grade classroom during math time. These factors may have contributed even more to her feelings of exclusion by her classmates.

In our counseling sessions, Olivia was excited and always eager to use any art material to express herself. She liked to use big canvases, such as large sheets of paper or the chalkboard. She would start on her art right away and often step back from her work without prompting, to decide what she wanted to add to her art next. During our time together, I wanted to help Olivia in B-SMS 2 (Self-discipline and self-control) and B-SMS 7 (Effective coping skills). Whenever I noticed Olivia thinking about her work, I would say, "It looks like you are thinking first before you add more colors and shapes." In doing so, I wanted to reinforce skills that she already possessed relating to self-control and self-discipline. She would not respond, instead, she remained quiet and focused on her art until she was done.

In our first few sessions, I focused on emotion identification and regulation. In one session, I had her work on mini-drawings to illustrate what different emotions looked like to her. She was able to name different emotions, such as mad, sad, scared, happy, and drew out pictures of herself feeling these emotions. When I asked her to draw out what she felt at that moment, she drew herself as happy again with a big smile and A+ symbols in the background. She asked if she could have another sheet of paper, and she drew herself bigger with a larger smile, larger flowers, and A+s all around her, as seen in Figure 3.9. When I asked what the A+s meant, she stated that it was her getting good grades. I asked her, "From looking at your art, it looks like this person in this drawing wants to do well in school, and that it makes her feel proud. Would you say that's true?" She nodded as she kept looking at her drawing, and then added more flowers. Though she often stated that she didn't care about school, it appeared in her art that school was important to her, and she wanted to do well.

In our last sessions, I continued to note how focused, calm, and confident she appeared when she was making art, especially when she added details. I wanted to let her know about these abilities she possessed, in hopes of her seeing that she could translate them to other settings, such as the classroom. Eventually, Olivia was found eligible for special education services to address her academic

Figure 3.9 Olivia expresses the emotion of happiness in her drawing.

needs in reading and math, as well as longer-term counseling services with the school psychologist. To ease the transition, I asked Olivia if I could share her artwork with the school psychologist to demonstrate her skills and her interest in expressing herself through art. Olivia smiled and agreed happily. In doing this, the psychologist was able to have an understanding of who Olivia was in visual form before their first session, and continued to work on her goals through art.

Case Study: Ethan

Ethan, an eighth-grade student, often came to school appearing tired and disheveled. His teachers expressed concern for his well-being, as he would put his head down on his desk most of the time, and as a result, he was falling behind in most of his classes. He was a student who received special education services for a learning disability; however, due to lack of participation, it was difficult for him to benefit from these services. One of his teachers informed me that he was self-conscious as he was unable to read at the level of his peers and did not want to be called on to read aloud when he was in the general education classroom. The special education team was in the middle of exploring interventions that would help him with his reading skills, and Ethan was going through the eligibility process to receive long-term counseling services on his Individual Education Plan. There was also a home/school coordinator who was assisting the family with additional resources for food, clothing, and apartment searches. During this time, he was referred to a small group to increase his social skills and connect with others struggling academically. However, his minimal participation in group activities and interaction with others warranted a change to short-term individual school counseling.

One of the ASCA Standards that I wanted to address in individual school counseling was Mindset 4, self-confidence in his ability to succeed, and planned to use his art as a critical part of the process. In sessions, he was polite and participated in the art more than he did in the small group. However, Ethan spoke minimally, and when he did, it was with a low voice, much like a whisper. I explained to him that during our time together, I could catch him up on some of the activities within the lessons that I provided in the classroom. "Graduation Day" was one of them, which he was able to complete with one-on-one support. He appeared to be overwhelmed at first by the art directive. I recalled that in previous artwork he created in a group, he demonstrated minimal mark-making, so I recommended that he could start with a smaller space around his graduation silhouette. I folded down the paper to reduce the size, and when asked if he preferred the smaller space, he agreed. He then started working quietly on the drawing (see Figure 3.10).

When he was done with his drawing, I asked him, "What do you think of your artwork?" He looked down at his drawing and nodded his head. Next, I asked him if he was happy in his picture as I pointed to the smile, and he nodded again and appeared to look more closely at the face he drew, as though he didn't realize he drew himself smiling. I asked if the people in the background were his family members, and he nodded again. I thanked him for participating in the drawing and informed him that he seemed to be focused on it and was able to complete his picture, to which he nodded again. Acknowledging these factors during this brief period of time with him was an effort to boost his self-confidence and pride in his work. He was given the opportunity to see that he can do something, that he is competent and able to complete an assignment at hand.

In another session, Ethan worked on his coffee cup as part of his classroom assignment for art class (see Figure 3.11). This art directive came as an idea after collaborating with Ethan's art teacher, who was working with the classroom on creating coffee cups to hang in a local coffee shop in the school's neighborhood. The art teacher shared that Ethan did very minimal work in class, if any at all. I suggested to the art teacher that Ethan work on his cup in a session with me. She then provided the template of the cup, paper, and drawing supplies. She also agreed to provide participation credit as part of his grade if he completed the assignment during his time in counseling.

Figure 3.10 Ethan draws himself on graduation day.

Figure 3.11 Ethan's design for a coffee cup.

Ethan started on his cup without hesitation and when he completed his cup, I asked once again, "What do you think of your artwork?" He nodded his head. I noted again his ability to complete the task at hand and pointed out the details and different colors he used in his cup. He didn't respond much verbally to my feedback, but once again, I observed him to look more closely at his art in response. I then shared with him again that he appeared focused and that he seemed to enjoy completing his drawing, with the hope of his knowing that he had these abilities, and to help him translate this one day into the classroom.

The opportunity to complete something that didn't involve reading and writing for Ethan helped him recognize that he can complete a task while creating something unique. When school can often remind students that they are not doing well enough, the counseling session was designed so that Ethan can start to recognize the abilities that he does possess to support him academically, and, in turn, pave the way to building his confidence. He eventually received services for longer-term counseling per his Individual Education Plan. With Ethan's consent, I shared his artwork with the social worker, who was going to continue counseling with him, to visually showcase his strengths and capabilities, and to support him in his growth moving forward.

3.6   Conclusion

In this chapter, we discussed how art therapy can be seamlessly integrated into school counseling practice. We saw how the art demonstrated student learning related to the ASCA Student Standards. The art served as a vehicle to process their growth with the help of the school counselor and address mindsets and behaviors relevant to three domains: academic, social/emotional, and career. Intentionally using art to teach the core standards was also demonstrated through the tiered levels of support - classroom instruction, small group, and individual counseling - meeting the student's specific needs for learning in a way that the student could respond to.

3.7   On to Part II

In the first part of this book, we laid down the essential groundwork needed for school counselors to understand the impact of integrating art therapy approaches in school counseling practice. Having explored the foundations of art therapy are and how art therapy approaches align with the ASCA Professional School Counseling Standards and ASCA Student Standards, we will now look at how school counselors can practically integrate the therapeutic benefits of art into school counseling practices.

References

Allensworth, E. M., Gwynne, J. A., Moore, P., De La Torre, M., UChicago CCSR's publications and communications staff, Krone, E., McDaniel, B., & Puller, J. (2014). Looking forward to high school and college: Middle grade indicators of readiness in Chicago Public Schools. https://consortium.uchicago.edu/sites/default/files/2018-10/Middle%20Grades%20Report.pdf

American School Counselor Association (2021). ASCA Student Standards; Mindsets and Behaviors for Student Success. Alexandria, VA: Author.

Collaborative for Academic, Social, and Emotional Learning. (2023, March 3). *What is the CASEL framework?* CASEL. https://casel.org/fundamentals-of-sel/what-is-the-casel-framework/

Collaborative for Academic, Social, and Emotional Learning. (2025, January 16). *What does the research say?* CASEL. https://casel.org/fundamentals-of-sel/what-does-the-research-say/

Erikson, E. H. (1958). *Young man Luther: A study in psychoanalysis and history*. New York: Norton.

Erikson, E. H. (1963). *Youth: Change and challenge*. New York: Basic books.

Farrington, C. A., Roderick, M., Allensworth, E., Nagaoka, J., Keyes, T. S., Johnson, D. W., Beechum, N. O., & University of Chicago Consortium on Chicago School Research. (2012). *Teaching adolescents to become learners: The role of noncognitive factors in shaping school performance: A critical literature review*. University of Chicago Consortium on Chicago School Research. https://www.kipp.org/wp-content/uploads/2016/11/Teaching_Adolescents_to_Become_Learners.pdf

Hatching Results. (2024). Multi-Tiered, Multi-Domain System of Supports (MTMDSS). https://www.hatchingresults.com/multi-tiered-multi-domain-system-of-supports

McLeod, S., Ph D. (2024, January 25). *Erik Erikson's stages of psychosocial development*. Simply Psychology. https://www.simplypsychology.org/erik-erikson.html

Sutherland, J., Waldman, G., & Carolyn, C. (2010). Art therapy connection: Encouraging troubled youth to stay in school and succeed. *Art Therapy: Journal of the American Art Therapy Association*, 27(2), 69–74.

Part II

Implementing Art Therapy Approaches in School Counseling

Chapter 4

Setting the Stage to Create Art

Now that we've gone through the history of art therapy and how it is aligned to the ASCA School Counselor Ethical Standards and the ASCA Student Standards, you might be asking the question: Where does a school counselor even start introducing art as part of their practice?

This chapter will review setting the stage to create art, including structural considerations, developing an inviting space, and art materials and their implications. Where it all starts, though, is with you. If you're a licensed school counselor, you have the education, experience, and skills to provide counseling services in the school setting. You have likely adopted theoretical orientations to ground your work and may have already incorporated the art-making process in your practice. We will explore the additional factors that contribute to an optimal environment in which to create art and use it to maximize its benefits for students.

4.1 Structure and Creative Freedom: Striking a Balance

For students to gain the most from art therapy-based interventions, such as increased self-confidence, motivation, participation, and overall engagement in school, the art-creating environment must first and foremost feel safe. This is the case regardless of whether you are introducing art as part of a classroom lesson, in a small group, or individual counseling sessions, and should be considered before setting up the physical space. What does this mean exactly? For a school counselor, this means setting up a structured yet welcoming space that is inclusive and non-judgmental. Each student should feel secure in creating their art pieces freely and confidently. Establishing a space where all art and the time spent making it are respected, results in the students feeling seen and heard. After all, art created by the student is essentially an extension of the themselves, and must be treated with care.

I've found in my practice that the key is always to let students know that, unlike art class, their art would not be graded, judged, or compared in any way. It can be reassuring for them to hear that there is no real right or wrong way

DOI: 10.4324/9781003430940-7

Table 4.1 Helpful phrases to encourage art-making and creativity

Key Phrases to Integrate Art Therapy Approaches in School Counseling
"Everyone's art will be unique, just like we are all unique." "This is not an art class, you won't be graded." "There's no right or wrong way to create your work of art." "Stick figures are ok!" "Choose colors that stand out to you." "Focus on the movement of lines, shapes, forms, as you create them." "You can keep your art or I can hold on to it for you. You get to decide."

to develop their art piece and that each student's work of art will be unique. Informing students that doing so would be impossible since each person is different from one another, and as a result, the art produced will be different as well. This approach will emphasize their unique personalities, interests, experiences, and backgrounds. This plays an important role in helping them demonstrate who they are and what's important to them, all while their learning through art is supported. Table 4.1 provides phrases that I use to introduce the art-making process to students. They are also useful in redirecting students, should they become hesitant or doubtful in the middle of the art-making process.

I've discovered through my years of integrating art therapy approaches that once the groundwork is laid out to emphasize a non-judgmental approach, there is a sense of relief among students. So much of what students do is "judged" in a way, whether intentional or not, by school staff, parents, or their peers. Whether that be through grades or test results, what high school or college they get into, or the clothes they wear, the friends they make or don't make. It comes as a sense of relief to be welcomed in a space, and there is an appreciation to play, take risks, and be unique.

4.2   Student Role in Creating Safe Spaces

Establishing a safe space involves students understanding how they play a part, especially in a classroom or small group setting, where they will be making art with others present. Doing this emphasizes a means for students to develop Mindset 2 of the ASCA Student Standards: sense of acceptance, respect, support, and inclusion of self and others in the school environment (American School Counselor Association, 2021). Additionally, this allows the students to learn and practice Behavior Social Skill Standard 2: building positive, respectful, and supportive relationships with students who are similar to and different from them (American School Counselor Association, 2021). In this section, student art, language use, and caring for art materials, as they relate to creating a structure for creative freedom and the responsibilities of all those taking part in the art-making space, will be discussed.

I've found the easiest way to facilitate students' contribution to creating safe spaces for art-making is to align with schoolwide expectations. For example, at my last school, the schoolwide expectations were "Be Respectful," "Be Responsible," and "Be Safe." This was part of Positive Behavior Interventions & Supports, a Tier I Universal Program to address social/emotional learning and establish a safe and welcoming school culture and climate. Using a structure already in place schoolwide helps to make the messaging consistent in all spaces, including one where art will be created. Since students were already familiar with the language, they contributed to aligning school-wide expectations with the expectations in the art-making space.

During a first classroom lesson or individual or small group counseling session, I explain to the students that they will create art to help them learn and grow the skills needed to reach their goals. This can lead to a discussion, and the expectations can be written on a board or large paper. I will then ask what each school-wide expectation can look like when it comes to the art itself, the language used when discussing the art or art-making process, and taking care when using the art materials. As students provide feedback on what each expectation can look like in the art-making space, I can write it out for them to see. Table 4.2 provides an example of a poster of expectations developed by the school counselor and students participating in an art-therapy integrated small group session.

Table 4.2 Group norms aligned with school-wide expectations developed by the school counselor and students to include the art-making process

	🐾 Tiger Paw Expectations 🐾		
	Be Respectful	Be Responsible	Be Safe
Student art	For classroom and small groups: Work on your own art (unless it's a shared art piece)	Put your name on your art	Keep finished artwork in a safe place (take home, leave it with the school counselor, and display it only with permission from the student/artist)
Language use	Questions and comments should help others learn about themselves and others	Remind yourself and others of the expectations during classroom lessons/ counseling sessions to use appropriate language	Confidentiality – keep information about what others shared about their art and other information private
Art materials	Share art materials *Treat materials with care	Place materials back where they belong Keep materials on the table or where art is made	Use art materials for its purpose (mark-making, sculpting)

If you don't have schoolwide expectations, there may be rules that the students follow based on the structures put into place by their classroom teacher. This is a great time to collaborate with teachers to find out what respecting materials in the classroom looks like and translate that into students' time with you as the school counselor. Alternatively, you can ask the students themselves what they believe makes a safe place to create art, and take the discussion from there, ensuring that all factors are covered to make that space happen.

4.3 Respecting the Art, Respecting the Student

A major factor in creating a safe space for art-making includes informing students about how the art will be used and what will happen with their art. Again, we are taking into consideration that the art is an extension of the student, and first and foremost belongs to them. As a result, the student decides what will be done with the art. In a classroom setting, I inform students they are able to keep their artwork once they are complete. If I would like to display the art on the bulletin board, for example, the "Dream Career" drawings from Chapter 2, I will ask them if this would be ok and give them the choice to leave their art with me before the class period is over. Once the bulletin board display is taken down, I return the art to the owners.

As far as small group and individual counseling, just as with any other session, I explain that the art will be kept confidential, meaning that information about the art shared in the session will remain between those in the session. Ethical Standards will be described more at length in Chapter 5, but it is important to note here to set up a safe space for the art-making process and have the student understand this before participating.

4.4 Language Use

Because the art will be used for students to learn more about themselves and others, the way students communicate about the art and the art-making process is essential in helping students feel safe to share their art with others. Sharing their art in this space allows for their voices to be heard along with the voices of others. When beginning a session, I inform students of the importance of the language they use towards their own art. For example, I advise them to catch any self-judgmental thoughts, such as "I'm not an artist," or "I can't draw," or "Everyone else is a better artist." Rather than focusing on these negative statements, I encourage students to be mindful of self-judgmental thoughts, how they may affect their ability to create, and not to become enveloped with them, as these thoughts are not helpful to the task at hand. I teach them the strategy to label these thoughts, acknowledge them, place them on a cloud, and allow them to float away. As a student is accepting of their art, they are accepting of themselves.

Once students learn helpful and positive language toward their own art, I share the importance of language use when there is a discussion and sharing of each others' art. Naturally, for students as well as adults, a response to another's art is "Great job," or "That's pretty!" I encourage students to state their observations of another's art and ask any clarifying questions. If something stands out to them in another person's art, I encourage them to ask more about it. At the same time, students should be informed that they may share their art in a way that feels comfortable to them. More details on how to process the student art will be described in Chapter 5.

4.5   Caring for Art Materials

Maintaining the quality of art supplies in the creative space helps to optimize an environment conducive to art-making. As students learn their part in respecting art materials, they recognize the value these tools have in helping them liberate their thoughts, emotions, concepts, and ideas. And, by emphasizing a shared responsibility for everyone in the space, they recognize the importance of keeping the materials in good shape so they last long enough to use in upcoming sessions, and for other students to use.

Once the development of expectations is complete, they can be written on a board or hung up poster-style to serve a a visual resource of the factors that contribute to a safe space to make and process art. The school counselor can use it to refer back to, especially if students start to steer away from the expectations.

4.6   Collaborating with School Personnel

Collaborating with teachers and other staff can help you establish a structure to integrate art therapy approaches in school counseling services. By informing them of how art will be used in school counseling services, you may garner support and receive valuable feedback as they see the students daily. As teachers can tell you about what students have been learning in the classroom, you may be able to tie art therapy approaches in lessons to align with the current learning objectives. The start of collaboration can lead to a discussion on how the art will be used to foster and enhance student learning.

For example, if you are going into a classroom to co-teach a lesson, it's recommended to meet with the teacher to emphasize that the art will be used in a non-judgmental way, and reviewing with the teacher the setup, structure, and how art will be discussed. You may reference the language used around discussing art to create a culture that is inclusive and acknowledges all students as artists in their own right. You can inquire what art materials are already available within the classroom, and how the teachers set structure around using them. Do they have an established way to obtain materials? By table? Row? Are there enough materials for each student? If not, do they share with the student across from them or seated next to them? The idea is to follow a routine and structure around creating art that students are accustomed to, emphasizing the predictability and safety within this environment. If they don't have art materials readily available, you will need to plan on bringing in the necessary art supplies based on the lesson.

Being able to collaborate and consult with the art teacher is especially helpful when you'd like to integrate art therapy approaches in your school counseling program. One, you may be able to co-teach lessons during the art period. Two, you can get an understanding of what medium the art teacher has covered with students, translating those mediums into your school counseling services. For example, knowing that students have been painting with acrylics, or using pastels, or have been designing a cup as described with Ethan in Chapter 3, this may ease the use of art in sessions with the school counselor. I have been fortunate as well upon my collaboration with the art teacher to receive art supplies from them after knowing about my school counseling program goals. This was particularly helpful when I needed the additional supplies for larger groups of students when providing classroom instruction.

Up until this point, we've discussed creating an environment for students to feel safe in the art-making process. Establishing a non-judgmental atmosphere, informing students and staff how the art will be used, the language used during the art-making process and the art itself, how to maintain the quality of the materials, and collaborating with teachers for additional ways to set up a solid foundation have been covered. Next, we will take a look at how the physical space can set the stage for art therapy-integrated approaches in school counseling services.

4.7 Space Preparation: Creating the Place Where Art Happens

School counseling spaces vary from school to school and, unfortunately, some are less than ideal to hold a counseling session, let alone one that includes art-making. A large part of our job is advocating for our role and the ethical standards to have a safe space for students to receive counseling sessions. Advocating for a space for the creation of art can include informing the administration of the benefits of using art to enhance your practices. Once this space is established, whether it's a small office or an entire classroom; or anything in between, school counselors can transform the space, no matter the size, to facilitate art-making. What makes an art-making room come to life is all in the space preparation.

4.7.1 Furniture/Fixtures

While furniture and fixtures may be scarce in some school buildings, you will find that what's needed for art-making through school counseling services is not much at all. You may already have the following items available, or they can be donated by friends or family. Let's take a closer look at what to consider when preparing a space for students to express themselves through art.

4.7.2   Tables and Chairs

When working with a group of students, you should have enough tables and chairs for students to work and create their art independently before coming together as a group. There is sufficient space on the table for art materials to be spread out enough for students to view all that is available to them at once. Ideally, another student's art space is out of full view, fo example when students sit at individual desks or small tables. This allows them to create art based on their decisions rather than copying those of others (Wadeson, 1987). Make sure that all tables and chairs are stable and fix any wobbly legs. Because you have art materials, this will minimize them rolling off the tables or, in the case of paint, being spilled onto the floor.

4.7.3   Fixture for Cleanup

If you have a space with a sink, you have struck gold! Cleanup would be feasible, especially when working with paint. Having a place to obtain water and clean brushes quickly helps with time. If that's not possible, you can have a large jug of water ready to go when the students are going to paint for the session. You can then dispense the water after the session is over at the sink in a different location.

4.7.4   Storage

Ideally, you will have space to store art supplies. Whether this is in the form of cabinets or shelves, it is helpful to store away any extra materials that will not be used on a given day, keeping the focus on the materials being used in the immediate session. Additionally, students may opt for you to keep their artwork after a session, you will need a space to store the art. Since art made in a session should be kept confidential, unless agreed by the student to be displayed, the art should be stored in a place where only the counselor has access. More on ethical considerations on student art will be discussed in Chapter 5.

4.7.5   Art Cart

If storage in the space is limited, a mobile "art cart" can be used. As school counselors, it's important to have materials that make sense and are transportable for ease as they relocate from different spaces throughout the day. It has been the most efficient piece of furniture I've used to transport materials from the school counseling office to the classroom or a different location to run a small group.

Figure 4.1 An "Art Cart" in the school counselor's office.

See Figure 4.1 depicting a school counselor's art cart. It provides ample space to store art supplies in an amount that is not overwhelming. Materials that I maintain on the art cart will be described later in this chapter.

Let There be Light

Providing sufficient lighting for students to engage in the creative process helps them see the progress they are making on their art. They can see the possibilities of the art medium – such as the colors, texture, and forms – and be able to marvel at the artwork they've produced and all the details within. In my experience, I haven't been as lucky in having large windows in my counseling offices to take advantage of the natural light. However, artificial light from ceiling lights has worked adequately. However, if it's still difficult to see, you may consider bringing a desk or floor lamp to provide additional lighting.

Another consideration regarding lighting is where art will be stored or displayed (upon student consent). To minimize fading, stray away from locations where harsh sunlight will hit drawings and paintings. To prevent damage to artwork, especially clay sculptures, storage locations should be away from heat vents and radiators.

A Note about Music

Having the equipment to play music in the background while students create art can enhance the art-making process and increase focus. In smaller spaces, such as school counseling offices, and working with individuals or a small group of students, a device to play music – laptop, desktop, phone – with built-in speakers should suffice for sound. For a larger space such as a classroom, in addition to a device to play music, having speakers that amplify the sound for all of the students to hear would be ideal.

The therapeutic benefits of music on mental health and well-being are worth reading in addition to this book, and research has shown that music can add to the calming, motivating atmosphere (Raypole, 2023), enhancing the art-making process. You can play music recommended by the students, especially music that celebrates a student's cultural background. Alternatively, you can play popular or trending music, but finding instrumental versions can help students focus without the distraction of lyrics. Overall, you should use your professional judgment on whether or not the music being played helps students participate in the art-making process.

Visual Inspiration

School counselors should be aware of and be inclusive of all art-making processes, no matter how different they may be from one another. Students who are in a classroom or small group may see others creating art in a physical way, using a lot of movement and large strokes to create their art. Other students may take a different approach, creating small, lighter marks on their paper. What I've found in these spaces is that students may look around and make sure that how they are approaching art is the "right way," inhibiting their ability to start on their art at all.

In addition to using encouraging language outlined in Table 4.1, it can be helpful to have visuals that inspire creative expression, no matter what that looks like. This can be in the form of posters with inspiring messages for art-making. You may also write out quotes from famous artists. For example, to emphasize the message to students that using colors and simple shapes in their art can have significant meaning, I had Georgia O'Keefe's (n.d. as cited in Mellor, 2018) quote on the board, "I found I could say things with colour and shapes that I couldn't say any other way – things I had no words for," and a print of one of her abstract paintings that interpreted her experience of flowers. Other ideas include having a mirror in your room with messages around it that celebrate their individuality that you may already be using as a school counselor, such as "You Matter" or "Be Yourself, Everyone Else Is Taken." There are also posters available in teacher stores that promote creativity, and you may create your own, as I did in my previous school. Figure 4.3 shows examples of this.

Figure 4.2 Visual inspiration for art-making displayed in the author's old school counseling office.

4.8 Making the Art Materials Engaging

Much of the art therapy-based directives and prompts encourage students to make their own choices, fostering independence and creativity in their art. They are asked to choose colors, art mediums, and tools that speak to them. For this reason, it is important that they can see all of the materials at once that are available to them. I've often seen in different settings that students and adults alike will take one colored pencil out of the box, then place that pencil back in, take another one out, and repeat.

For example, you could take the markers out of the box and set them up on the table before an individual or small group counseling session. When students enter the room, they can see all the color options, encouraging them to engage with the activity by picking the color that appeals most to them. This is especially helpful as the actual duration of an individual or small group session can be brief due to the time spent gathering students from the classroom, and then making sure they return to class on time as agreed upon with the teacher.

Having all the markers, pencils, or other mediums and tools out and easily accessible makes them more inviting. For example, one teacher that I worked with had all of the markers and colored pencils organized on shelves by color. This setup contributed to the inviting nature and accessibility of the materials. If this is not the case and sets of art mediums are passed out in boxes, encourage students to take them out so they can see all of the colors to choose from. Having all of the options out, including other supplies, such as brushes of different sizes, makes them easy to grab. If you have an art directive that includes selecting a sticker to draw around, pre-cut images of animals to create an environment for, or sequins or other embellishments to choose from, lay them out in the middle of the table. This could be the table used to facilitate small group sessions, or a larger table in the classroom where students can take turns to choose their art materials. When setting up the space for exploration, there is a playfulness and freedom of choice in the materials, which can make the start of creating art fun and exciting. More times than not, I had adult school staff coming by my office excited about seeing art materials just as much as students were. See Figure 4.3 of an example of art materials displayed and ready for use.

Now that we have discussed the larger space and atmosphere when it comes to making art, let's take a closer look at art materials and their implications. Much of the art materials may have been ones that you've already used with

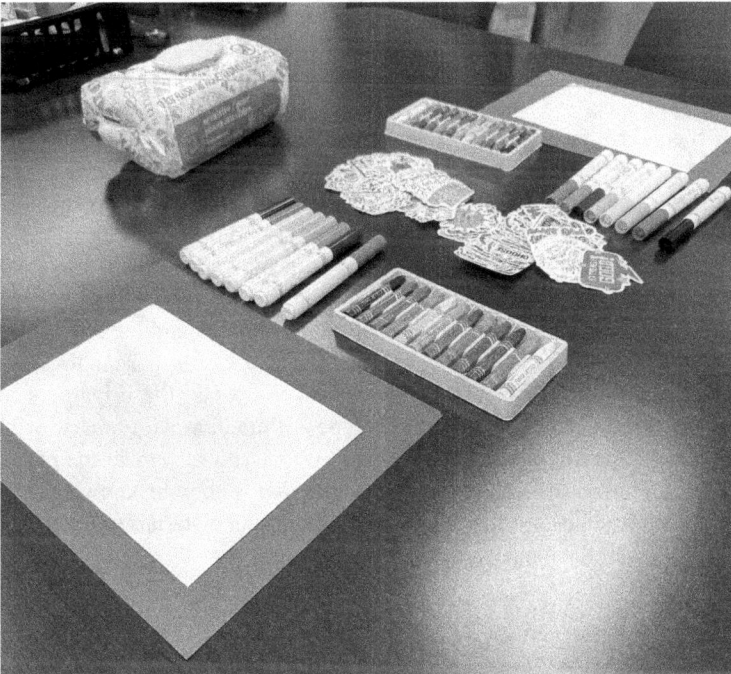

Figure 4.3 Art materials laid out and ready to use.

students. Understanding the characteristics and implications of different art materials, from the art medium, paper used, and tools, can help you use them intentionally and effectively with your students.

4.9   Art Materials and Implications

I remember stopping by another school counselor's office one day to pick up a form I needed. She had a student with her at the time, who was engaged in watercolor painting. Though it was a quick exchange to respect the student's session, I had enough time to notice that the student was painting on brown construction paper that had started to buckle, and the paint colors on this paper appeared duller than they did in the paint pan. Granted, I didn't have the context for the session at the time, perhaps the student chose that specific paper for its properties. After all, the student did not appear frustrated by the buckling, nor unsatisfied with the appearance of the colors, and she seemed to be enjoying the process. But I couldn't help but think how a simple switch of paper could enhance the student's painting experience. With paper specifically designed for watercolor paints, with its ability to absorb and handle water, a student can witness the unique properties of the paint come to life – how the paper receives it, blends with other colors, and how it reacts when more paint or water is added. The idea is to maximize the possibilities of the art materials. Whether it's the type of paper, paint, or other material, we can optimize the students' experience so that they can arrive at their completed art as a reminder of this experience.

Art therapists have an educational background in visual arts, making them aware of the properties of a diverse set of art materials, from the different types of medium, paper, and tools to create certain effects. However, if you do not have this background, there are simple ways to increase familiarity with art materials that most likely have already been used in your own art, or with your students. The best way to know the materials and their characteristics is to experiment with them yourself. Though you've likely used markers and pencils before, try using them with intentionality, paying attention to your response to the medium. Notice how the art medium leaves marks on the paper, the brightness of the colors, the effects of blending different types of medium with others, or notice the fluidity of the medium, or the rigidity. When you recognize the properties of the art materials beforehand and combine that with your knowledge of the student, you're in a better position to determine if the materials would be appropriate to use with the students to meet their goals.

4.9.1   Cost-Effectiveness and Practicality

Before I go into the materials, it's important to note that the materials I've chosen are cost-effective yet quality enough to help students make impactful and unique art pieces. More often than not, budgets are limited, and finding out what supplies are absolutely necessary can keep costs down. Opting for student-grade art materials, for which you can get recommendations from the art teacher, or shopping in the sale and clearance aisles at the art supply stores, you will find how much art can be created within a budget.

The art materials mentioned in this chapter are also practical. Given the time constraints when collecting students for a small group, or getting ready for a classroom lesson, or arriving at a team meeting on time after a session, we know that the last thing we need is to do extensive clean up given the limited time-frame. I don't recommend anything advanced, such as oil painting, for a few reasons: cost, clean-up, and limited experience with the medium.

Materials listed in this chapter are easy to transport as needed and, even more importantly, easy to clean. All of the art materials that are discussed here have been available in my office on a table and/or on my art cart. From there, I've been able to integrate the art therapy directives and lessons described later in this chapter. Now let's take a look at art materials and mediums in more detail.

4.9.2 Paper

The choice of paper all depends on the art directive and what medium will be used. There are directives where using white copy paper for a student to create a quick drawing will suffice. Typically, this type of paper is sufficient if pencils, thin markers, or pens will be used. Other directives that include art media such as oil or soft pastels, would be optimized with mixed media paper to impact the brightness and texture of the medium. Mixed media paper can withstand the blending of different types of medium, such as pastels applied with more pressure to obtain a concentrated color. Construction paper in assorted colors, in addition to white paper, can work nicely for pastels as the background will have a different appearance and impact on the art. Watercolor would need paper specific to these paints as they are typically thicker than most other papers in order to hold water. With the thicker quality, it is able to hold the medium without tearing, warring, or buckling easily. Whatever the type of paper, I always suggest having a variety of sizes available. The choice all depends on the directive and the goals of the session or lesson.

4.9.3 Art Medium

Art medium is the material used to create the art, such as markers, pencils, pastels, and clay, and can be described in terms of the ability to control. For example, there will be more control with pencils and markers than with paint. Paints such as watercolors or acrylics are more fluid and considered less easy to control. Like paper, the choice of medium depends on the art directive and what you want the students to achieve, combined with your knowledge of the students. On one hand, markers or pencils may be frustrating for a student who wants more freedom and movement, especially if they want to cover more ground in a shorter amount of time, as they can with paint. Or, you may have a student who can become easily frustrated with watercolors, as they are more fluid and can bleed into other colors on the paper. Watercolors are also transparent, so building up colors for thickness would not be as achievable as it would be with acrylic paints.

You can see the list of mediums and properties of each to consider when using with students in Table 4.3. As mentioned earlier, the best way to become familiar with their potential is to use them with intention before introducing them to students in an art therapy-based approach integrated into your practice. Even if you have used pencils and markers before, experiment with them on different types of paper, and the same for other mediums. Notice your own experience while creating art, and use this to inform your practice when introducing art materials to your students.

Balancing Art Medium and Structure

While it is important to ensure respect for the materials, the freedom allowed with each art medium must also be considered. The characteristics of art mediums are discussed in detail in this chapter; however, let's take a look at the use of clay and pastels as it relates to this section.

Clay comes to mind as school counselors express concern over having students who have displayed an inability to respect materials in other school settings. They worry that it will be another object that could be used to throw around, or be something that could create mess in the space. Hence, they do not provide clay for the students to use at all. Although counselors should use their professional judgement, offering clay as a medium for students could also be seen and used as a learning opportunity for them. A benefit of using clay comes from its tactile nature – it can be flattened, twisted, torn apart, and put back together – giving a sense of liberation which many students could benefit from. This is where the importance of establishing boundaries prior to introducing art materials in the session comes into place. When I've used clay with students, I will have an additional supply, such as a lunch tray, or a placemat. I inform the students that they are allowed to work with the clay freely but it must be within the boundaries of the tray or placemat. This serves two purposes: (1) to keep the clay off of other areas and the space tidy and (2) to serve as a metaphor of how they are free to express themselves through their art, but in a way that is within boundaries. Both purposes help the student and others safely share the space.

Pastels, whether oil or soft, are delicate and can be easily broken into pieces. I've had some students apologize when they have broken them accidentally, and I can see that they genuinely feel bad about it. From then on, I made sure to demonstrate the use of pastels so students can notice their characteristics before they use them. Helping students recognize the art medium's characteristics will help alleviate the worry of resources being broken. You can note that pastels are fragile and can easily break, and that's what makes them unique, allowing for blending, smearing, and layering, all of which they can explore in their art.

Table 4.3 Art cart materials, levels of control, and considerations when using with students

Art Medium	Level of Control	Considerations
Markers	High	Students are likely familiar with markers and can be easy to use for most students without the need for demonstration or technical assistance. Use for quick or mini drawing directives.
Colored pencils	High	Like markers, students may have experience with colored pencils. They offer control in its use and offer the ability to gain more detail in a drawing. Colored pencils do not easily spread and cover as much paper as pastels or paint.
Oil pastels	Moderate	Oil pastels offer more vibrant colors than crayons. Students can use their fingers to blend the colors. They are easily breakable since they are less dense than crayons which allows for blendability. Students can spend a session simply experimenting with colors, layering them, and blending them while engaging in discussion.
Soft pastels	Moderate	Soft pastels are just that. This characteristic makes them easily blendable with their powdery, chalk-like consistency. Shows up well on dark paper. Can create spontaneous and planned-out pieces of art.

(Contiuned)

Table 4.3 (Continued)

Art Medium	Level of Control	Considerations
Acrylic paint	Moderate to low	Paint in general is more fluid than the previous art mediums mentioned, thus characterized as having less control. It can blend with other colors to create a new color, while covering more space in less time than markers or pencils. Acrylic is also good for risk-taking. When it is dried, a student can paint over parts of their painting or add to their work. Can be used on canvas and to paint dried clay.
Watercolor paint	Low	Less control than acrylic paint, as the paint uses water to create different hues of a color, and they bleed into other spaces depending on the water amount on the brush and paper. Use watercolor specific brushes as these brushes are less dense than others and hold more water. Good for mindfulness practices as students can be present and observe colors bleed into one another, and how wet watercolor paper creates a different effect when painted on than a dry piece of watercolor paper. This could be beneficial for students who need help with easing anxiety, as they can be mindful of the paint and notice the effects when it is brushed onto the surface.
Air dry clay	Low	A benefit to using air dry clay is the opportunity to create a permanent three-dimensional piece that a student can paint to their liking. It also offers a tactile experience that other material may not offer, making it a low control medium due to its malleability. Students can flatten, roll, pinch, and dent the clay, allowing for expression through the clay.

4.9.4 Other Art Materials

Other materials I keep either on the art cart or on hand are listed in Table 4.4:

My go-to for quick and efficient cleanup of hands and tabletops is baby wipes. This is especially helpful if there isn't a sink in the room or nearby. They can

Table 4.4 Additional helpful materials for the art-making process

Tools	Embellishments/Images	Clean-Up
• Child-safe scissors • Glue (liquid and stick forms) • Acrylic and watercolor paint brushes, various sizes • Mason jars (to hold water for painting) • Plastic plates or lids (to serve as a palette) • Lunch trays or Placemats (to keep medium within boundaries)	• Emoji stickers • Images of animals (stickers or cutouts from magazines) • Inspirational quotes (stickers or from magazines) • Glitter • Sequins • Scrapbooking paper and Stickers	• Disposable aprons or large t-shirts • Babywipes • Multipurpose spray cleaner • Paper towels • Disinfectant wipes

quickly wipe off pastels, clay, and paint until students can get to a sink, allowing for time to reflect and process the art as soon as it's completed. For art directives that involve paint, you may have disposable aprons or old oversized t-shirts (that can be washed later) for students to wear to protect clothing.

In my office, I had a small round table that had different-sized multi-media paper, pencils, and markers readily available, along with emoji and other stickers. I also kept these materials accessible on my art cart, along with the other art materials. I had art materials that are often used, such as markers, oil pastels, pencils, and multi-media paper on the top two tiers, and others not used as often toward the bottom, such as glue, watercolor paper, embellishments, and clay. Any additional materials were stored in a cabinet where I can easily access them to switch with ones on the cart or replenish the cart as needed.

As time goes on, you will make your space and art cart based on your experiences, ideas, and how your students respond to different types of materials. For example, school counselors have told me about how mini paint canvases have been fun and engaging for students in their counseling sessions. Due to the size, these canvases allowed for completed paintings in a single session with easy clean-up. Others have found sales on origami paper that students used to make collages or to draw the designs from them onto another piece of paper. Once you start engaging with more art materials in your practice, you will discover that the possibilities are endless.

Now that we have discussed the setting of the space for art-making, as well as the materials and implications, let's discuss how we can use them to integrate art therapy approaches.

4.10   Let's Start with Art

Several art therapy-based directives have already been discussed through case studies in previous chapters and how they address ASCA Student Standards. Much of what I've used was based on previous experience in art therapy and ideas that were prompted as I worked with students. For example, the "Graduation Day," and "Dream Career" drawing objectives described in Chapter 2 were ideas that came about to make learning more dynamic, relatable, visual, and motivating than what the curriculum had provided at the time.

The art directives described in this chapter may address specific goals at the start, but it is important to note these same directives may address other student needs as they arise organically. In order for our practice to be effective, we should be flexible and ready to address what is brought forth by our students. As such, I would caution against considering art therapy discussed here or any other text to be strictly prescriptive. All too often, there is a search to find a quick activity to resolve a challenge, but working with students is hardly that easy, nor should the interventions be thought of in that way.

Therefore, the directives in this chapter are not part of an exhaustive list. Many other ideas come up when using art with students. That's the beauty of using art; creativity blooms, ideas are sparked, new art directives are developed and facilitated, and ultimately, the students benefit. In other words, the work does not end here. This is only the start of your practice becoming more creative as you become open to the possibilities.

Finally, while some of the art directives described have a lesson plan available in the Appendix based on ASCA Lesson Plan formats, this chapter will aim to help you understand why and how a particular art directive is applied, whether or not there is an accompanying lesson plan. The goal is to increase your understanding of how art can help a student grow, and often, this cannot be achieved solely through reading the lesson plan.

Continuous Line Drawing with Oil Pastels

This particular art directive is based in part on Florence Cane's Scribble Technique (Cane, 1951) to help those creating an art piece release inhibitions and embrace spontaneity during the art-making process. This directive can help to facilitate freedom, challenging the concept that their art should look a certain way. For this reason, this art directive is helpful to use in the first session in individual and small group counseling, or as an opening exercise before a classroom lesson. In any setting, this art directive can minimize the need for their art to look "pretty" or "right" as may be the case in an art class that emphasizes technical skills and aesthetics. This will also emphasize the uniqueness of each drawing, setting up the space for future art-making to be inclusive of all art, and in turn, all students.

In this directive, students will be led to use a black marker or pen and move it across the paper in a continuous line without lifting it off the paper. It may be helpful to demonstrate this to the students before they begin. After about one minute, the school counselor can demonstrate how oil pastels can be used and added to their line drawings. I've found that even though students may have used oil pastels before, they haven't experimented with them in the following ways:

- Layering the colors on top of each other.
- Using fingers to blend the colors.
- Smearing the oil pastels across the paper.
- Using a plastic utensil to scrape the oil pastels lightly from the paper to create texture or designs.
- Removing the paper label from the pastel, turning it width-side down on the drawing paper and shade in color, allowing for more space to be covered.

Having students participate in this simple art directive emphasizes the liberation in creating art, being present in the art-making process, taking risks and exploring the medium, and overall taking part in a nonjudgmental experience that can more often than not be calming and relaxing in nature. In Figure 4.4, you can see student drawings using this art directive. This exercise can help the student open up and create connections with the counselor or with a group of students. However, how to ethically process art will be discussed further in Chapter 5. You may view this art directive in Lesson 4.1 in the Appendix.

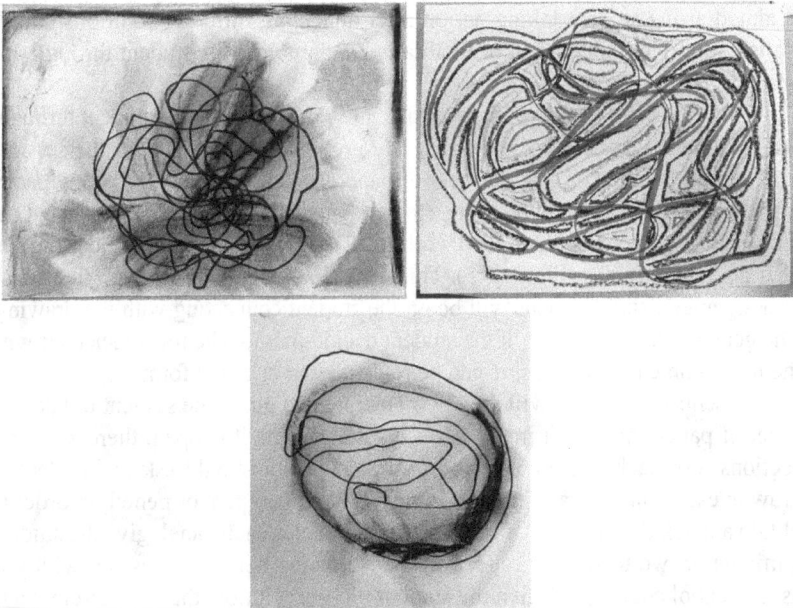

Figure 4.4 Students from various grade levels created continuous line drawings with oil pastels.

A few other art directives that can help with releasing inhibitions and invoke a sense of play and freedom that I've used in my experience include:

- **Paper Bag Sculpture** – Use a brown paper lunch bag and the materials inside it to create a sculpture (the bag can be filled with yarn, tape, stickers, pipe cleaners, etc.)
- **Clay Exploration** – Pinch, roll, tear, put back together, flatten, and see what sculptures unfold
- **Oil Pastel Resist Watercolor Painting** – Create designs with a white oil pastel on white watercolor paper. Then add watercolor paint to the paper and notice the oil pastel marks resist the paint.

Now that we've gone through a few art therapy directives that can encourage artistic freedom, we will discuss art therapy-based directives as they relate to counseling theory. We'll start with Solution-Focused Brief Therapy.

Bridge to a Miracle: A Solution-Focused Approach

A simple way to integrate art into your already existing practice is to apply it within the theoretical orientation that grounds your work. As school counselors, we are trained in Solution-Focused Brief Therapy, as it serves to resolve challenges students face in a shorter period of time compared to other theories. It is aimed at the student taking action after analyzing different solutions, and it starts with the school counselor facilitating and guiding the student through this process.

In a "Bridge to a Miracle," the school counselor will guide the student throughout the drawing process to create a visual to refer to during and after the session. This can all be done on a wide sheet of paper, such as an 11" × 17" copy paper, often accessible in a school building. Rather than the instructions being printed out on the paper as typically done for a worksheet, the school counselor guides the student through the steps (Figure 4.5). This way, the process will feel less like a task or assignment, and the focus will be on the student connecting with the drawing. The goal would be that even if the student decides not to take the finished art with them, the content of the session can be remembered in visual form.

The school counselor will then demonstrate and guide the student to take the sheet of paper and fold it into a tri-fold so that when it is open, there are three sections. For each step in Figure 4.5, the counselor should ask the student to draw in each panel for a minute or two with a marker, pen, or pencil, in order to obtain a quick drawing. When the student completes each panel, give the student a minute or two to silently reflect on their drawing before processing with you as the school counselor. When the student picks a solution, they can circle it and draw themselves crossing the bridge.

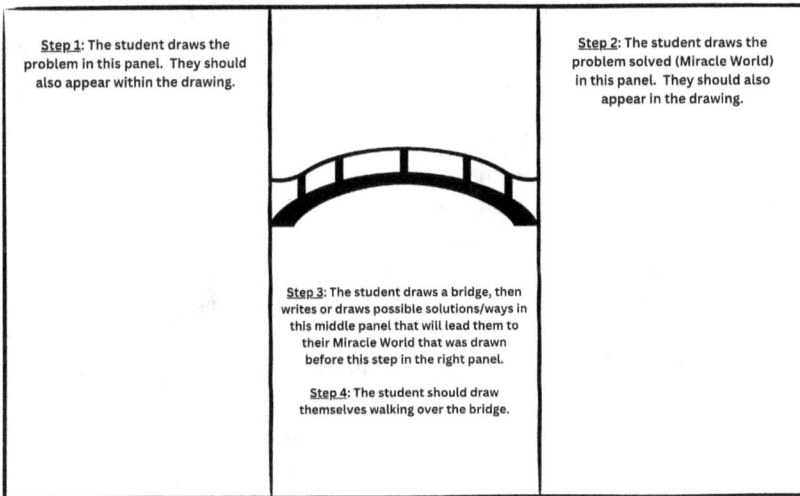

Step 1: The student draws the problem in this panel. They should also appear within the drawing.

Step 2: The student draws the problem solved (Miracle World) in this panel. They should also appear in the drawing.

Step 3: The student draws a bridge, then writes or draws possible solutions/ways in this middle panel that will lead them to their Miracle World that was drawn before this step in the right panel.

Step 4: The student should draw themselves walking over the bridge.

Figure 4.5 Format for "Bridge to a Miracle" drawing.

An important part of the drawing is for the students to place themselves within it. In that way, they can see themselves in their "miracle" environment and describe how they would be acting, thinking, and feeling in that space, leading to a discussion of how they can be exhibiting those characteristics in the present day. From here, the visual can be used to discuss possible solutions that will take the student across the bridge from their current state to their miracle world.

Small Group Art Therapy-Based Directives: An Adlerian Approach

In using an Adlerian approach, the art can be used to bring awareness to commonalities among a small group or a classroom of students, facilitating the process of students getting to know their peers on a deeper level and increasing a sense of belonging (Cedeno et al., 2024). Using art as a unique extension of each person, students can develop social interests and gain a sense of purpose in the group. Referring back to the "Dream Careers" classroom lesson mentioned in Chapter 3, a school counselor can bring awareness to how each career contributes positively to society as a whole. I would often emphasize that students can look forward to success in their future careers, but that would look different for each and every one of them. And that would make them all, in a unique way, positive, contributing members to society, which are often cited in school and school counselor program vision statements.

By using an art directive to make the group create something collaboratively, the art can highlight the unique contribution of each person, illuminating the significance of their collaboration. This information can then be used to process and lead a discussion on how this can be translated into the school setting at large and other social settings. More on processing art using an Adlerian approach will be discussed in Chapter 5. A few examples of collaborative art-making directives include:

- **Group Sculpture** – With your group, create a sculpture out of newspapers, packing material, and masking tape.
- **Mural Painting** – Each group member has a different color of paint in their cup. They will paint on a large piece of paper for 30 seconds, and then move one spot over to start painting another 30 seconds. The mural is complete once everyone is back in their spot. Play music in the background to encourage movement in their brushstrokes and spontaneity.
- **Classroom Quilt** – Give each student in the classroom a 4 × 4 inch piece of mixed media paper. Ask each student to draw out a symbol, an animal, a flower, or whatever represents joy to them. Display the finished art next to each other in a quilt format for the students to see.

Free Art: Person-Centered Theory Approach

A school counselor could integrate art therapy approaches based on Person-Centered Theory, where the student creates art with little to no direction. Sometimes a student is not able to think of ideal situations or solutions to problems, and in these cases, the focus of these sessions should be to meet the student where they are. For example, if a student comes to your office upset and distressed, we know that based on neuroscience, the student will struggle to verbally express what is upsetting in the moment. Using a person-centered approach, you can give the student freedom to choose what materials to use and make a visual representation of their current state. In this case, the student can look at your art cart and choose their art materials. It is important to use the student's art with unconditional positive regard, a concept in person-centered therapy where the student and their art are accepted no matter what. This will help the student to feel at ease and unpack any overwhelming emotions.

The person-centered approach can also be used to provide the students with the freedom to create whatever they'd like and while doing so, the school counselor can be there to support the process. This is especially helpful after having several lessons or sessions with art directives, as this can allow them to use the skills they learned during this time and express themselves freely, choosing whatever art materials are available to them. Figure 4.6 shows a group of newcomer students who were part of a small group intervention, who asked to paint a mural together. Without any direction to do so, they included images of their home country, such as the national flags, beaches, sun, mountains, and palm trees. These particular students had been in the U.S. for over a year or two, yet it was evident in their art that the memories of their homeland were at the forefront. This allowed the

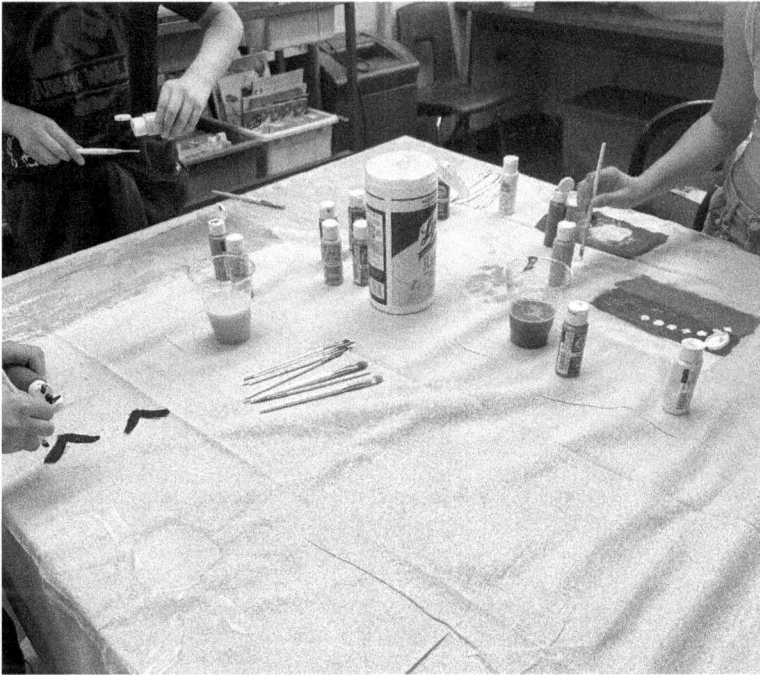

Figure 4.6 Students paint a mural with images from their home country.

counselor to acknowledge what is important to them, give space to share pride of their cultural background, and recognize their shared experiences.

Emoji Drawing: A Cognitive Behavioral Theory Approach

One of the most helpful and impactful art directives that I've used with students in individual and small group counseling is the Emoji Drawing directive (Arroyo, 2020). These drawings can be created with markers, colored pencils, emoji stickers, and white mixed media paper in either 5" × 7" or 4" × 6." If you don't have emoji stickers, you may find images of emoji online and print them out. For the size of paper, this is typically smaller due to the scale of the emoji stickers and the aim to contain strong emotions. The art directive for the student is simply to pick an emoji sticker that best reflects how they feel, and to draw around it. Students can draw for 10–15 minutes. See Figure 4.7 for instructions you may have pre-printed on paper or as a slide for students to refer to.

Though this art directive was originally developed for students in a state of distress, it has since been developed into a lesson that can be used to better

EMOJI DRAWING

Instructions:

1. Pick one to three emoji stickers that best represent how you feel right now
2. Place your emoji stickers anywhere on your paper
3. Draw around your emoji to emphasize how you feel right now
4. You may add lines, shapes, scribbles, stick figures, words, etc.
5. Create as much as possible in the space around your emoji
6. There is no right or wrong way of how your drawing should look

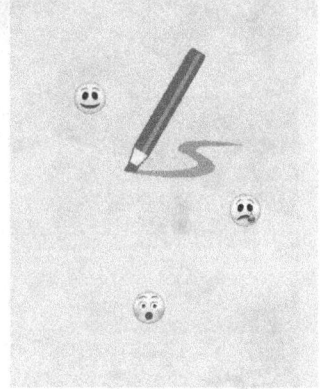

Figure 4.7 Instructions for the "Emoji Drawing" that can be presented to students during a session or lesson.

understand different emotions, especially strong ones, before they come about. Using Cognitive Behavioral Theory, beliefs behind the emotions can be identified and the school counselor can help disrupt incorrect or unproven thoughts that the student believes to be true. The time taken to reflect on these beliefs allows for better understanding of their emotions. This helps students to realize that by changing their negative thought patterns, their emotions and actions change based on more positive and rational thought patterns.

To allow for students to discuss different emotions, the lesson was developed to further explore them in response to various challenging situations that often happen during the school day. Students are given a scenario, and then asked to pick 2 or 3 emojis that best represent how they would feel based on the scenario. After each scenario, a discussion among the students is held to discuss thoughts behind these emotions, and for everyone to share their point of view. This offers an opportunity for the students to learn from one another and also help each other recognize any thoughts behind emotions that may be harmful or untrue. Once the scenario discussion is wrapped up, they have the opportunity to select emoji stickers that represent how they are feeling in that moment, create art around it, and again share and reflect with others. See Lesson 4.2 "Emoji Drawings" in the Appendix.

Many times we hear how important it is for students to regulate their emotions, but by having the opportunity to express, identify, and understand a range of them in a safe way, they are more likely to manage these emotions in a positive way. See Figure 4.8 for examples of student emoji drawings.

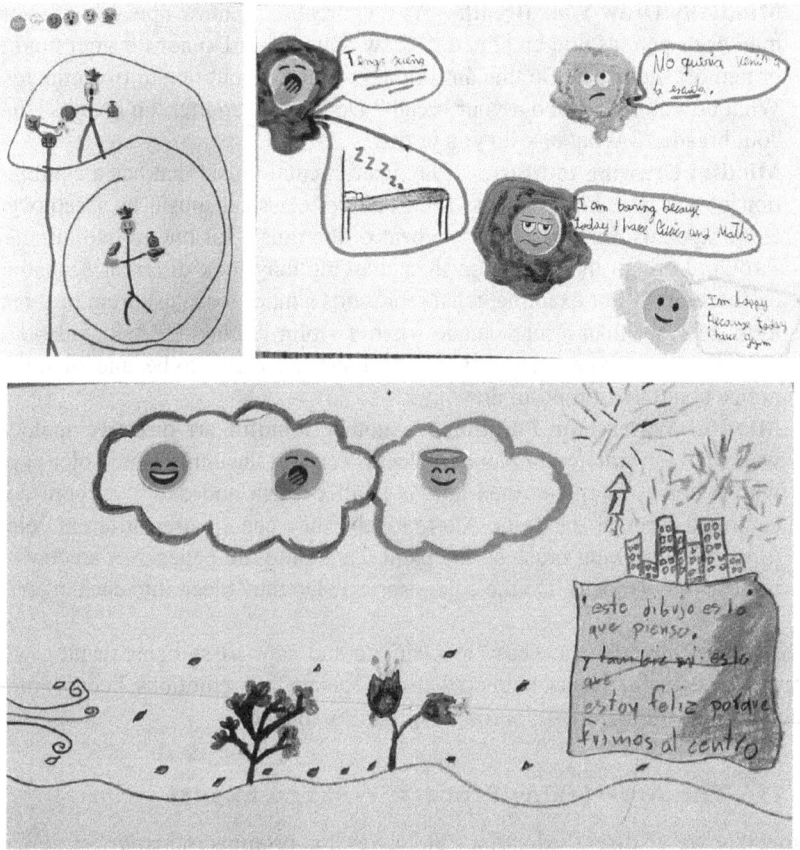

Figure 4.8 Student emoji drawings to express how they feel.

Mindfulness-Based Art Directives

The use of mindfulness in schools has increased in recent years, and growing research has shown positive effects on student learning and general classroom behavior (Sapthiang et al., 2018). In my last school, a mindfulness-based program was used as a Tier I SEL program accessible for all students. The curriculum was trauma-informed and designed to improve mental focus and emotional well-being for the entire class (Calm Classroom, n.d.). With this established, I was able to integrate art therapy approaches through mindful art to enhance core mindfulness skills of being present, paying attention, and having compassionate awareness (Vo, 2015). A few "go-to" art directives to enhance mindfulness practices, whether to start a classroom lesson, or an individual or small group counseling session, include:

- **Mindfully Draw Your Breath** – As you breathe in, draw upward with your marker or pen, as you breathe out, draw downward. Do not lift your marker or pen off the paper. Do this until time is called (about one to two minutes). What do you notice about your breath? Do you see shorter "in breaths" than "out breaths"? What else do you notice?
- **Mindful Drawing to Music** – Play instrumental music that has a combination of low and high tempos, for example, classical music by Beethoven. Have students draw to the tempo/beat of the music for one to two minutes. Explain to them that marks on their drawing may look different depending on the sounds. For example, what represents a mark for a fast drum beat may look different than a mark made when a violin is playing. Ask students to reflect on their experience, how mindful they were able to be, and what they notice about their mindful drawings.
- **Mindful Watercolor Painting** – Another mindful art directive includes working with watercolor paints. Students can wet the entire watercolor paper with a brush. They can then take a smaller brush and dab in a more concentrated form of the paint. Alternatively, they can splatter different colors of paint by flicking brush so the paint lands onto the paper. Ask students to notice what happens. Do the colors spread? Do they bleed into each other?

Mindful art directives are easy to facilitate and support students dealing with trauma or stressful events, helping them to regulate their emotions, become more focused, and ultimately supporting their ability to learn.

4.11   The Art-Making Process: What to Expect

Now that we've discussed various directives and prompts to inspire art-making among students, let's take a closer look at the "during" part of the art creation. This is a critical period for school counselor support as the students become engaged with the art, exploring the materials, discovering the possibilities, and coming across technical challenges. A number of responses can happen, whether it's frustration with the medium, second-guessing their choices, and not knowing how to ask for help. Here we will explore some key points that can impact the art-making process, and how to address them.

To Art or Not to Art: School Counselor Participation

School counselors have asked me whether or not they should create art along with the student, or whether they should simply observe. Ideally, the student will be the only one creating art, giving the school counselor an opportunity to assess the student's process in decision-making, attention and focus, need for technical assistance, and, in a group of students, how they are able to work alongside others. Observing the student or group of students can be a part of the school counselors' gathering of valuable information needed to accurately assess what the student needs. For example, a school counselor can observe whether they have difficulty choosing colors on their own, appear worried or confused, or unable to start altogether. These observations can help the school counselor identify appropriate next steps in their practice.

There can be a range of student reactions when introducing art into school counseling services. This can depend on developmental level, experience with materials, and trust, which are only a few factors that may impact their participation in making art at the beginning. Some students will dive right into the materials and not worry about whether their art will be judged by me or anyone else. On the other hand, especially in a group or a classroom, there may be some hesitancy to creating art as students seek acceptance by their peers and fear embarrassment. However, there may be other factors contributing to their lack of participation, and the counselor would need more context. Is the student tired, hungry, or scared? In this case, taking care of the primary needs would be prioritized rather than the art-making.

In some cases, the student may seem hesitant or insecure about how to proceed, as lack of direction of what is "ok" to create or what they should or should not draw can inhibit them. In this case, I may start on my own art and start filling in space with color, or drawing simple lines to model the process. I may inform them that the color I picked stood out to me in the moment, and that's why I picked it, and for now that I was placing it on the paper to see where it goes. This role modeling for the student combined with the assurance that their art will look different than my own, others in the group, or in the classroom, may help them get started independently.

When I am creating along with the student, I will proceed at their pace, to not be ahead in the art process. Naturally, students are curious to see what I am working on rather than on their own work, or want to "copy". In response, I redirect them to take the time to create on their own, and time will be spent afterwards to share our art and ask each other questions. If a student seems hesitant at first, some time will pass when they will notice their peers starting on their art and becoming invested. They begin to be curious about the materials in front of them and eventually start on their own art and become just as invested in it as their peers.

Technical Assistance

There may be times when students will need technical assistance with the art medium. Keeping in mind that counseling is based on learning mindsets and behaviors and to facilitate expression rather than to learn an art skill, the school counselor may assist with the student's art in a way that stays true to the student as the artist (Wadeson, 1987). This is in contrast to making suggestions for the art piece, or advising what the student should do next with their art. The school counselor can help with gluing pieces of paper or objects together if the student is having difficulty, but the student will need to guide the school counselor on where and how the objects are glued together. As another example, if the paint is too runny, the school counselor can show the student how to dry off the brush on a paper towel or sponge if there's too much water or paint on it and prompt the student to practice doing this on their own.

Student Participation

There are times, no matter the setting, where the student will finish the art ahead of others, and in a one-on-one session, they may finish before the school counselor. From my experience, often students will return to their art once they realize how others in the room are invested and focused in the creative process. If this is not the case, you can certainly check in with them, reminding them of how much time is available for them to continue developing their art piece. If there is a lot of blank space in their drawing for example, you may ask them if this was intentional, and part of how they wanted their art to appear. If it was not intentional, you can encourage the student to think about adding additional lines, shapes, designs, animals, people, etc. From there, they can decide if they'd like to continue. When reminded of their freedom to choose how their art is going to look, I've seen students dive right back in, and end up still working when time is called to wrap up the art-making process. Finally, if the student is not willing to continue, that is ok too, as we don't want to push participation, as the art should be seen as a choice by the student. Perhaps the student will want to play a game to warm up, or simply talk about what is going on.Use your professional discretion and instinct on how to proceed with your student.

4.12   Practice and Reflect

Before going on to the next chapter, I recommend the following activities for greater understanding and connection with the context of this chapter.

1 Explore any of the art mediums discussed in this chapter, whether that be oil pastels, watercolors, or clay, and create free art.
2 Complete one of the art directives listed in this chapter.

Once your art piece is complete, reflect on your work silently or by journaling. You may answer the following questions as part of your reflection:

1. Which directive did you pick and why?
2 What thoughts and feelings came up for you while you were creating your art?
3 How do you see your students benefiting from the art therapy-based directive?
4 How do you feel right now?

4.13   Conclusion

Now that we have set the stage for art, including establishing safety, setting up the physical space, exploring art materials, discussing art directives, and addressing challenges and responses, the next step is to process the art with the students. In the next chapter, we will start to understand how to process the art intentionally with your student to maximize its benefits in school counseling practice.

References

American School Counselor Association. (2021). *ASCA student standards; Mindsets and behaviors for student success*. Author.

Arroyo, L. (2020, September/October). *The art of school counseling*. ASCA School Counselor, 20–23.

Calm Classroom. (n.d.). Educators – Calm classroom. *calmclassroom.com*. Retrieved March 1, 2025, from https://get.calmclassroom.com/

Cedeno, R./ Torrico, T.J. *Adlerian Therapy*. [Updated 2024 Jan 11]. In: StatPearls [Internet]. Treasure Island (FL): StatPearls Publishing; 2024 Jan-. Available from: https://www.ncbi.nlm.nih.gov/books/NBK599518/

Cane, F (1951). *The artist in each of us*. Pantheon Books.

Mellor, M. (2018, September 13). *Georgia O'Keeffe: Mother of American Modernism - Arts & Collections*. Arts & Collections. https://www.artsandcollections.com/article/georgia-okeeffe-mother-american-modernism/

Raypole, C. (2023, May 30). Music and studying: it's complicated. Healthline. https://www.healthline.com/health/does-music-help-you-study#articleHistory-wp-2305070

Sapthiang, S., Van Gordon, W., & Shonin, E. (2018). Mindfulness in schools: A health promotion approach to improving adolescent mental health. *International Journal of Mental Health and Addiction, 17*(1), 112–119. https://doi.org/10.1007/s11469-018-0001-y

Vo, D. X. (2015). *The mindful teen: Powerful skills to help you handle stress one moment at a time*. Instant Help.

Wadeson, H. (1987). *The dynamics of art psychotherapy* (2nd ed.). John Wiley & Sons, Inc.

Chapter 5

Got Art, Now What?

5.1 The "Art" of Processing Student Art

A key question I get when training school counselors on integrating art therapy approaches into their practice is this: What happens once the art has been created?

It can seem daunting to know how to move forward once the art has been made. You have gone through the process of setting up the stage for art, offering the materials and art directives, and now the students have put down their pastels, paintbrushes, or other tools, and are looking to you for guidance. Now, what? As a school counselor, how can you help your students process their art to assist them in developing the key mindsets and behaviors according to the ASCA Student Standards?

In this chapter, we will explore the "art" of processing student art. We will begin by looking at why it's valuable to process student artwork, creating a non-judgmental and safe environment for sharing and reflecting, as well as the ethical considerations needed when discussing student art. We will look at how we can assist the students in interpreting their own artwork, increasing their self-awareness and self-identity, as well as continuing to support the students in developing these key mindsets and behaviors. Through the use of case studies, we will see examples of processing art in different settings, such as in the classroom, in smaller groups, and during individual counseling sessions. From there, we will look at how different counseling theories can be implemented when processing artwork, such as Solution-Focused Brief Therapy, Cognitive Behavioral Therapy, and Person-Centered Therapy. Above all else, this chapter will outline how school counselors should treat the student's artwork with respect and acknowledge that the student is the only interpreter or meaning-finder of their art.

5.2 Ethical Considerations and Student Art

Before we dive into *how* to process art, it's crucial to understand *why* it's valuable for school counselors and students, especially when working toward the

DOI: 10.4324/9781003430940-8

ASCA standards. But, most importantly, school counselors need to acknowledge how to process art ethically, encouraging confidence in the students rather than self-consciousness.

From their therapeutic training, a school counselor has the skills to build strong, trusting relationships with their students through dialogue, relatability, and empathy. This serves as the foundation for integrating art therapy approaches into practice, as these skills maximize the benefits that art brings into the space. A major benefit to this is that the art serves as a representation of the students that is separate from themselves. This provides a reference for the school counselor to recognize student strengths or discover behaviors that serve as barriers for students in reaching their goals.

When processing their art, school counselors can help students make meaning out of the imagery, and the artwork can act as a point of reference to help the school counselor gain an understanding of who the student is. The artwork opens a window into the student as a whole and not just their behavior that is shown outwardly, such as a student who struggles to listen, who talks back to teachers, or "doesn't try hard enough." Through their artwork, the student will likely reflect who they are beyond those descriptions. Simply put, the art is an extension of the student, and just as you would ask questions of the student to gain more insight when you are using traditional talk therapy techniques, the act of processing art means you use the art in the same way.

However, it is important to reiterate that the only interpreter of the art is the student. The art should not be used to psychoanalyze or elevate the session to a clinically therapeutic one, as that would be beyond the scope of the school counselor's role. The student's art is meant to express, communicate, and serve as evidence to the students themselves that they can create a work of art, whether finished or not, representing something visual and tangible that didn't exist before.

It's important to note that in small group or individual counseling, what a student shares through their art should be considered confidential information. This information should be treated much the same way it would be treated if it were shared verbally or in written form. The counselor has an ethical obligation to protect the privacy of the student and balance this with their safety and well-being, the legal rights of parents and guardians, legal requirements, school district policy, and so on. Explaining the limitations of confidentiality to students as you normally would in any other session, should include what that means for their art.

When it comes to the physical piece of art, the student is the owner and should decide what happens to the art after processing it in the session. They can decide to take it with them after the session. If they want it displayed in your office, you should inform them that others come through your office and may see their art, especially if their name is on the art. From there, they can decide if they still want it displayed. The alternative would be that the art is displayed with their name covered up. Or, the student may opt to have you, the counselor, keep it in a safe place inaccessible to others. In this case, the counselor can ask the student at the end of the school year if they'd like to take it home. If they decide not to, you can keep it as part of the student record and follow district policy accordingly. In any case, as in traditional counseling, you can seek out consultation with other school-based mental health professionals or administrators regarding the confidentiality of student art.

5.3   Art in School Counseling vs Therapy

A school counselor asked me after one of my conference presentations, "Where is the line between staying within school counseling and clinical therapy when it comes to the art?" I responded that the school counseling role and ethical standards remain the same whether we are introducing art, music, play, or movement into our practice. When referencing the student's artwork, we use it to gain information to support their learning in a short period of time, and also to help the student understand what can help them with their social-emotional, academic, and career skills. If you come across information that would warrant a referral to more intensive therapeutic services, then the school counselor should move forward as if they were using talk therapy techniques. Addressing family of origin issues, significant trauma, and mental health diagnoses is not treatable with school counseling. To put it simply, we ask students how they feel or think about things all the time. Having them respond through art is providing another means to communicate other than speaking or writing. And in many cases from my experience, much information has been shared through art that led to referrals for the student and family for services available outside of the school.

It is also important to note that, even though art can demonstrate meaning and significance, once the art is completed, there is no need to push the student to create meaning in that given moment. As described further in the chapter, another important yet simple aspect of what to do now that we have art is to acknowledge participation in the process and accept the art as it is, which, in turn, demonstrates acceptance of the students for who they are.

5.4   The Core Principles of Processing Student Art

Regardless of the setting, there are some core principles or best practices to adhere to when processing student art in order to promote growth in the ASCA Student Standards. As you will see, much of what was discussed in the previous chapter on setting the stage to create art will be reviewed here, as the idea is to maintain the structure from the beginning of the lesson or session until the end. This includes: (1) maintaining safety and trust while the student shares about their art; (2) sharing what you observed as the school counselor during the art-making process with the student, and; (3) the use of non-judgmental, inclusive language throughout the session or lesson.

As discussed in Chapter 4, it is incredibly important to allow the student to share their art in a way that feels comfortable to them. I've found in my practice that a student will provide the information, whether solely through the art, verbally, or both, at the level they feel comfortable sharing. An important aspect in helping students feel comfortable processing and sharing their art is ensuring that students stick to the classroom and group norms as discussed in Chapter 4. If there is any veering off of these expectations, the school counselor should re-direct students back to them when art is being discussed. Art is a representation of self, so ensuring respect and care toward it throughout providing school counseling services is crucial. The main idea is the ability to "see" the whole student, using art as a means to do so. We can serve as another set of eyes to see other things about their art, in a non-judgmental, accepting, and patient way.

5.4.1 Observing and Responding to Art

A simple start to processing the art is to share with students what you observed while the students created the art. If students appear relaxed and focused while creating the art, I will share that with them. I will also share if I noticed whether they seemed to think carefully about the images they chose to add to their collage, or the colors that they chose to fill their paper. I do this to point out that they can exhibit these behaviors. Many times, when students are referred to school counseling, it is because they haven't demonstrated skills in the classroom or other settings in the school. Simply pointing this out to the students can help them recognize that they already have the ability to demonstrate skills such as critical thinking and decision-making, or B-LS 1 and B-LS 9 of the ASCA Student Standards, which contribute to academic success. This sets the foundation to have the students transfer these skills to other settings. For example, in a class that they might find challenging, such as math, science, or reading, they can practice approaching these subjects in a calm state, and take the time to think carefully when academic work becomes difficult. They can also recognize that creating art, or any other activities that provide relief from stress, can be done in other settings as well, depending on the situation, to help them cope positively. When they become overwhelmed with homework, they can take a break to draw in a sketchbook, for example, to relieve stress. After acknowledging their participation in the art-making process, there are a few general tips and prompts that I use, whether it's a classroom setting or within individual or small group counseling.

Another key point in responding to art relies on the ability to stay attuned to your students' needs, and respond accordingly. For example, a school counselor in the pilot program recognized that a student in the group participated in continuous line drawing with oil pastel art directive, and created a drawing of his best friend from his previous school (Figure 5.1). This student was a newcomer student and his living situation had been unstable for the past several years,

Figure 5.1 A student's drawing of his best friend from his previous school.

having migrated to a new country, went from one temporary living situation to another, leading to several changes of schools. This was a moment for the school counselor to process what was on his mind and to acknowledge the many transitions he's endured in his young life. Being able to process this in a group with other students with similar challenges helps to alleviate stressors and feelings of isolation. What may have been expected was to discuss abstract art, which often happens with this art directive, but turned out to be an opportunity for students to share significant experiences and people in their lives.

5.4.2 Use of Language

To maintain a non-judgmental environment to reflect on the art, my first tip to use for yourself as a school counselor, and to share with students if in a group setting, is to avoid any type of comments that provide a value of one piece of art over another. For example, comments such as "Great job!" or "That looks pretty!", or if students are sharing with a partner in class or in a small group, "You're a better artist than me!". These types of statements would deem one student's art as "better" than the other, which would go against helping the student feel safe in expressing who they are in their art, as unique or different from others. Additionally, feedback such as this while processing the art may give the student a sense that their art on one particular day would be better than on a different day, creating a sense of always having to create a "good" or "pretty" piece of art each time. The aim is to use the art for greater awareness and acceptance of themselves as well as their peers. This is consistent with maintaining that art created in the spaces with the school counselor is unlike being graded in an art class, but more for communication, self-expression, and experiencing the calming effects of art-making.

Instead, use dialogue, such as "This part of your drawing has a lot of detail to it." "Could you tell me more about the shape of your sculpture?" " I see that you used a lot of this color. Does it represent anything in particular?" Doing this helps the student to connect more with what they created and be the interpreter of their art. Additional prompts can be seen in Box 5.1. These statements and questions can be modified to meet the developmental stages of the students.

Prompts for Processing Student Artwork

Tell me about your drawing.
What was it like for you to create this?
Is there anything that stands out to you about your drawing?
How did you choose the colors and shapes in your art?
What does that person in your drawing think/feel?
How do you feel now?
What do you think of your drawing?
What common themes do you see in the group art?
What are some differences?

With these simple prompts, along with a safe, non-judgmental environment, the school counselor and student will see how art provides insight into who the student is, how they may relate to other students, and allows for their unique qualities to be celebrated. A school counselor using these simple prompts and questions about a student's art will soon see that many times it doesn't take a whole lot for the student to express what they need to share, even when they don't verbally expand on their art at all.

Now that we've reviewed some general pointers in helping students in processing their art, let's take a look into considerations when in different settings: classroom, small group, and individual counseling.

5.5   Student Art Processing in the Classroom

As explored in previous chapters, art therapy approaches are usually incorporated in classroom settings by school counselors as part of Tier I programming to reach a larger group of students and ensure they have access to learning the ASCA Standards. The art created in the classroom can be likened to a written reflection a student may write as part of further understanding of a novel they are reading in class, for example, but with art instead, they will share their thoughts in a visual form.

In a classroom setting, the students are among many of their peers when creating their art, and it is important to acknowledge the unique considerations to bear in mind when facilitating a lesson. This is to ensure the students meet their goal confidently when in a large group environment. Additionally, the classroom setting lends itself easily to supporting students in achieving certain mindsets and behaviors according to the ASCA Student Standards.

First, we should start by acknowledging that when providing classroom instruction, the dynamic will be different from facilitating a session with an individual or small group. The students will not receive the individualized attention from you as a school counselor, and therefore, there are unique factors to consider such as:

- Developmental needs of students and learning styles.
- Classroom routines that can be streamlined into processing artwork (i.e. classroom expectations).
- Students who need additional support or modifications throughout the class period.

Furthermore, it is important to root the art-making and reflection process in the mindsets and behaviors students can develop. The classroom setting lends itself easily to teaching and reinforcing the following mindsets and behaviors of the ASCA Student Standards (American School Counselor Association, 2021):

- M 2. Sense of acceptance, respect, support, and inclusion for self and others in the school environment.
- B-LS 9. Decision-making is informed by gathering evidence, getting others' perspectives, and recognizing personal bias.
- B-SS 2. Positive, respectful, and supportive relationships with students who are similar to and different from them.
- B-SS 4. Empathy.
- B-SS 6. Effective collaboration and cooperation skills.
- B-SS 7. Leadership and teamwork skills to work effectively in diverse groups.
- B-SS 9. Social maturity and behaviors appropriate to the situation and environment.
- B-SS 10. Cultural awareness, sensitivity, and responsiveness.

When I provide classroom instruction, no matter what the identified mindset and/or behavior that are identified for the lesson, I mainly ground my work with the Adlerian theoretical orientation, as it serves as a structure to bring awareness to commonalities, such as feelings of belonging and having a purpose (Cedeno et al., 2024) among the students. Through processing the art, I aim to help students identify their strengths, their personal goals, and a sense of hope or need for help, to foster a sense of connectedness with one another featured through their art. I am also on the lookout for encouragement they provide one another, such as sharing of materials, or asking for advice on their art, and I bring this to the processing session as something I observed to reinforce these behaviors. From this, let's see how this looks in practice.

Case Study: Student Art Processing in the Classroom

I was invited to provide support to a class of high-achieving high school students, as the advisory teacher expressed concern about their stress levels. The students were in their junior year right before final exams of the first semester. Their teacher informed me that many of the students started to feel overwhelmed and stressed due to all the work they had to get done, and how much their grades meant to college admissions. She informed me that a strength of the class was that they were a close-knit group, as many of them had the same advanced classes together since their ninth grade year. In response, I planned a lesson to focus on B-SMS 7, effective coping skills.

After setting the stage to introduce the lesson, "Stress Less, Art More," I informed them that I was aware from their teacher that many of them had been feeling stressed lately. I let them know that, especially during this time of year, it is understandable that they would feel under pressure and overwhelmed. I acknowledged their worry as a sign that doing well in school was important to them, but that today we would experience one of several ways to de-stress, according to research, and that is through art. I then discussed the purpose of the art as described in Chapter 4, assuring them it would not be part of a grade or used to judge technical art skills. I then led the students to complete the continuous line drawing with oil pastels art directive. Once they completed their drawings, I guided the students to pause and look at their work and asked the following questions (from Box 5.1) and reflect silently after each one:

"What was it like for you to create this?"
"Is there anything that stands out to you about your drawing?"
"How did you choose the colors and shapes in your art?"
"How do you feel now?"

Once I finished reading the questions, I shared with them my observations on their participation up until this point. I told them how focused and calm they appeared while working on their drawings. I then asked "How many of you felt that this was the case for you?". All of them raised their hands. I then shared, "I also noticed that you all looked at your drawings with curiosity, and some with surprise as I read each question." I asked if this was the case, and some students looked at each other, smiled, and then several, though hesitantly, raised their hands. Because I knew from the teacher that relationships were strong in this group of students, I led them to share their art with a partner. I presented a slide with the same questions I read out loud, and informed them that they were going to share their answers with a partner. I modeled how I would hold up my drawing in front of me so both myself and my partner would be able to see the drawing. I reminded them about the guidelines of using language to gain more understanding, rather than shorter statements, such as "Great job," or "You're an artist!" I stated, "Once your classmate is done sharing their answers, ask them any questions you may still have, or any comments or observations you would like to share with them."

Once they picked their partners and started to share their art, I walked around as they shared smiles, laughter, pointing to their pictures. After about 10–15 minutes, I called for everyone's attention back to me. I shared with them how I noticed that there was a lot of communication among them, and there seemed to be a lot of joy and satisfaction when sharing their art. I then asked if anyone would like to share about their experience of either participating in the art-making or their experience in sharing it with a partner.

After a few seconds of silence, one student raised their hand and said,

> At first I felt embarrassed about sharing it because it's just a line with some colors. But then I saw that my partner's work looked similar and we talked about how we chose our favorite colors to add to the lines.

I said, "Thank you for sharing. So you were able to learn a bit more about your partner and found some commonality through the art, as well as finding out their favorite colors." To which they stated, "Yeah, it was pretty chill."

From there, a few more students shared how they enjoyed doing the art and how they found the experience relaxing. Another expressed that they liked not having the pressure to make it look like anything. I thanked them all for sharing with me and for participating. I then led a discussion of how creating art, based on research, has a calming effect, and recommended that if they found this to be the case, they can always participate in art-making outside of class. I stated that, whether it was with a pen and a sheet of notebook paper, they can draw, doodle, or scribble, if it gave them a sense of calm when feeling stressed.

I then asked the students how else they can reduce stress in a way that is positive. One student stated that they could go for a walk, another stated that they called their best friend, and another stated that being a part of sports helps them relieve stress. I informed the class that this was valuable information and encouraged them to try any of these ways to cope with stress as shared by their classmates if they hadn't done any of them before.

I also emphasized the ability to connect with others. I shared that I noticed they seemed to enjoy themselves when connecting and sharing their artwork with each other. In doing so, I was able to emphasize and reinforce their ability to maintain positive, respectful, and supportive relationships with one another, or B-SS 2 of the ASCA Behavior Standards. This then led to a discussion of the importance of connecting with others when they feel overwhelmed and stressed, in order to feel heard, obtain support, and regain a sense of calm. I asked the students to identify trusted adults in the school building who could help them in times of need and receive additional support: teachers, counselors, social workers, coaches were all named. Before I ended the lesson, I informed them that the art was theirs to keep, and if it was helpful to display it somewhere to remind them of a calming experience and as a reminder that there are healthy and effective ways to cope with stress., or B-SMS 8 of the ASCA Behavior Standards.

The case above demonstrates one way to share and process art in the classroom to teach mindsets and behaviors. Another method I use for students to share their art with others is having them do a "Gallery Walk." Typically, I will use this method when the topic is less sensitive and personal than others (i.e. dream careers, ideal high schools or colleges), considering the number of students in the classroom, and the amount of time to process the art. In the Gallery Walk, I will have students either hang up their art around the room or leave the art where they are sitting, and students can walk around to view others' art. As they walk around, I ask students to pay attention to the following:

- What commonalities do you see in your classmates' artwork?
- What are some differences?
- What colors or images stand out to you or relate to you?
- What questions or observations do you have about the artwork?

Once the students finish the Gallery Walk, I will open the floor for anyone to share and to use the questions above as a reference. I will then share my observations and inform them if I noticed them looking around with curiosity, or if they had discussions around the artwork with each other, or if they seemed invested in learning about their classmate's art. I will end the lesson informing students that they can decide what they'd like to do with their art, whether they would like to keep the art, have it displayed in the classroom for motivation (per prior teacher consent) or leave their artwork with me, and I could keep it in a safe place.

Finally, there may be a time when students can use the art to practice their presentation skills. Oftentimes, students are asked to present in front of their classmates sooner than they are ready. Speaking about oneself in front of their peers can be a daunting, scary task, especially as students care deeply about the opinion of their classmates. The benefit of presenting with art is that the student can refer their audience to their creation, directing their peers' attention to their art rather than themselves. For instance, I co-taught a sixth grade class with the social studies teacher after learning that the students had started presenting in front of their classmates. As a means to help them obtain more practice, after the students completed their collages representing their career interests and shared them in smaller groups of 3 or 4 other students, they were given the opportunity to present their collages to the whole class. The smaller groups of students within the classroom stood at the front of the class together, and each one took a turn presenting their art. Presenting in this manner provided an alternative way to present their ideas rather than speaking directly to their peers the entire time. Not only did this bring an opportunity to practice presenting in front of a large group, but it allowed others to see more of who their classmates are through their art.

5.6   Student Art Processing in Small Groups

Similar to the classroom setting, the same ASCA National Standards listed above can be addressed in small group counseling using an Adlerian approach. Within the intimate, supportive setting, students can find common themes in each other's art while also learning from one another. This decreases the sense of isolation many in the small group may have felt, demonstrating to them that they are not alone in their struggles, but connecting with others experiencing similar situations.

As small group counseling is an additional layer of intervention based on the specific needs of the group, the school counselor needs to assess the students' needs through various ways to identify which mindsets and behaviors to focus on throughout the sessions. From there, they can identify an appropriate intervention and determine if integrating art therapy approaches will help them learn the mindsets and behaviors identified. Let's take a closer look.

Case Study: Student Art Processing in Small Group

Mrs. Gamara started a small group intervention with four fourth grade students who were referred to school counseling to improve their academic performance. All of the students received at least one D grade in a core subject (Reading, Math, Science, or Social Studies) at the end of week 5 of the school year. Upon consulting with students, teachers, and parents, Mrs. Gamara recognized they struggled for various reasons – from becoming anxious before tests, getting out of their seats when not receiving attention and then distracting others, to getting frustrated and giving up quickly on an assignment, or overall lack of confidence in being successful in school. Though the reasons were varied, Mrs. Gamara was able to identify the following ASCA Standards to focus on for this group of students: M 2. Sense of acceptance, respect, support, and inclusion for self and others in the school environment, and B-SMS 7. Effective coping skills (American School Counselor Association, 2021).

Mrs. Gamara's small counseling group integrated art therapy approaches to help students develop these mindsets and behaviors and also improve their academic performance in core subjects. The group adapted well to the first three sessions, establishing and following expectations as well as completing and discussing the art directives they were provided in the group. At this point, it seemed that the students were developing a trusting bond with one another, along with Mrs. Gamara.

One day was particularly difficult for Daniel in his ability to focus on the art directive and group expectations. While the other students were well on their way in making their "animal for the day," with clay, quietly focusing on how to create the shapes of their animals, and adding small details, Daniel became fidgety, and spoke loudly about his favorite rapper. At one point he stood up and sat back down several times, and in doing so he moved the table, causing the others to stop and look up at Daniel then at Mrs. Gamara.

Mrs. Gamara responded, "Ok, let's go ahead and move the table back so you all can continue working on your animals. It looks like you all are really getting into the details of your animals, such as whiskers and tails. Please continue."

One student responded, "Yeah I'm trying to do the ears on my cat and they got messed up." She then glared at Daniel.

Mrs. Gamara can tell that this student was upset and wanted to say something to Daniel. She responded,

I understand, I see where you started working on that. The clay is still wet it appears, so you may be able to smooth out what you started and work on the detail again. You can also use the spray bottle to add a little water to that section.

The student nodded. Mrs. Gamara reminded everyone about the small group's expectation of being aware of space and making sure everyone is respecting each other's art-making process. They all refocused on their animal, including Daniel, though he appeared frustrated. Mrs. Gamara then came around the table to ask Daniel how it was going with creating his animal.

"I'm trying to get my lion to lie down," Daniel said.

"Oh I see, that can be a little tricky, but let me see if I can help you," Mrs. Gamaran responded.

Mrs. Gamaran grabbed the same amount of clay that Daniel was working with to experiment and role model with a separate piece of clay. This was so Daniel could see the possibilities of shapes that could be made.

As Mrs. Gamaran rolled the body portion of the lion, she demonstrated to Daniel and stated,

What if we took this clay shaped like the body and lay it on the table so it flattens a bit, kind of like what would happen to the body of a lion when they lay down. We can also take a look at this photo of the lion as a reference.

Daniel proceeded to take the clay piece and mimic what Mrs. Gamaran demonstrated with her clay piece. He looked at it and then looked at the photo of the lion. He proceeded to mold the clay to liken it to the lion's body, then added the head he had created previously.

Figure 5.2 Daniel's clay lion lying down.

Mrs. Gamara asked, "What do you think?" Daniel responded, "It looks good." He then proceeded to add legs and the tail. He became as focused on his lion as the others in the group were on their animals, and completed it on his own. See his finished clay animal in Figure 5.2.

Before the end of the session, Mrs. Gamara shared that she observed in this session everyone working with the clay in a thoughtful and focused manner in order to achieve the look of the animal they wanted. She stated,

> *I noticed when you all started with a certain shape, if you didn't look like what you wanted, you tried other ways to create the shape you desired. I also saw you look at the animal reference photos to observe the details, and then recreate this on your clay animals.*

The students all looked at their animal pieces while she spoke about this, a couple of them moving their heads to observe their animals at different angles. Mrs. Gamara also directed the group to look at the other members' animals as well, to which they did with curiosity. Because the students needed to get to lunch, she wrapped up the session, explaining that the clay animals should be dry before their next session in a week, and at that time, they would paint them. She added they would talk more about their animals next week, including why they chose to be those animals, what it was like to make them, what their strengths and challenges are, and how they can all get along and help each other. Mrs. Gamaran then directed them to clean up their area and hands with baby wipes, before sending them to the bathroom to wash hands and finally escort them to lunch.

What happens in a smaller group setting often mimics what happens in the larger classroom or school setting. It becomes a microcosm, which helps the school counselor gain a better understanding of the challenges students face and be able to teach the ASCA Standards to address them. In this case, it seemed as though Daniel had difficulty with the art directive and, since he was working with a medium that is less controllable than the ones used in previous sessions, he was unable to express what support he needed in a positive way. It appeared he was frustrated with the clay, and in response started to speak on an unrelated topic and move around in a way that disrupted others' work. Mrs. Gamara role-modeled for Daniel what can be done by displaying a state of calm and focus, and taking time to discover what can be done with the clay.

Daniel's behaviors at the point where he started to struggle with his clay animal, combined with seeing the rest of their group involved in their art-making, may be aligned with Adler's theory of inferiority complex. This is where a student is overcome by an inferiority, whether conscious or not (Britannica, 2024), resulting in behaviors to gain attention from the social context, albeit to the disruption of the group. "Elementary school students can overcome insecurities developed earlier in their childhoods by learning to work in cooperation with others" (Wright, 2011, p. 187). In this case, Mrs. Gamara facilitated this in the session, redirecting members to the expectations of the group of being mindful of their space and that of others. Coupled with inquiring about Daniel's current state of working with his animal, and his desire to capture his animal to evoke the feeling he wanted to have, Mrs. Gamara was able to demonstrate learning in a way that respected others in the space. Mrs. Gamara's plan in upcoming small group sessions was to teach the students how to cope with frustration and feelings of insecurity in a positive way, and how to ask for help from others when needed all while being inclusive and respectful to others in the group.

5.7 Student Art Processing in Individual Counseling

Students who are referred to short-term individual counseling with a school counselor often struggle with a range of barriers to academic success, and these barriers cannot be addressed through classroom instruction or a small group setting. In an individualized setting, depending on what challenges the student faces, mindsets and behaviors are chosen to address them, and appropriate directives within the session are provided. A benefit to individual school counseling is that the time and attention needed to gather this information is more focused and, combined with the use of art, the school counselor can gain insight into the root cause of these challenges. For instance, say the student is fearful of speaking in front of others, or the opposite, they talk over others to gain the most attention. Whichever the case, a one-on-one setting with the school counselor and student is an opportunity to develop a safe, authentic rapport to assess and meet the student's needs, with the hope of being able to build skills to learn in an environment with others.

Without peers to share artwork with, it's critical that the student understands how to share their art with you as the school counselor. As mentioned in Chapter 4, I may complete my own art at the same time as the student if I believe that would encourage the student to participate. The following case study shows how I started the art processing with a fifth grade student named Melissa, who was referred to school counseling. Her teacher reported that Melissa seemed to have difficulty making friends, was mostly quiet in class, and would sit off to the side during recess and lunch. The teacher explained that when she asked Melissa if there was anything she needed, she would say that she was "fine." She was a recent transfer student and had changed schools multiple times in the past few years. In our first session, we completed the continuous line drawing exercise with oil pastels. Once we both completed our art, this is how we began processing it together:

Counselor: So, we are now going to share our experiences of creating our art pieces with each other to learn more about one another. We can also ask questions about each other's art. Keep in mind that you can share only what you feel comfortable sharing. Also, we're not in the classroom so there's no right or wrong way to go about this. It's like a regular conversation but with art. (Counselor and Melissa complete their drawings).

Counselor: Now that we're done, we can share what we worked on. Does that sound okay with you?

Melissa: (Nods her head yes)

Counselor: Would you like me to start sharing my art, or would you like to go first?

Melissa: You can go. (in a low voice)

(After sharing)

Counselor: Thank you for listening. I appreciate your interest in my art and willingness to learn more about what I created. Do you have any questions for me?

Melissa: Umm…it looks nice.

Counselor: Thank you. Was there anything that stood out to you? (counselor holds up the art)

Melissa: (points to an area of the drawing)

Counselor: Oh yes, I used a lot of pink there.

Melissa: That's my favorite color.

Counselor: Oh, I learned something about you today. Speaking of which, if you feel comfortable, would you like to share your art?

Melissa: (Nods and turns drawing so the counselor can see, but remains quiet while looking at it).

Counselor: Thank you for sharing. I noticed at one point you seemed to really get into your drawing. I notice a lot of details here in this part.

Melissa: (Nods head)

Counselor: Ah, and I do see pink in here.

Melissa makes a small smile.

Counselor: What was it like to create this drawing?

Melissa: (Shrugs her shoulders)

Counselor: Well, from the looks of it you seemed to know what you wanted in your drawing. The paper is filled with colors and shapes and lines.

Melissa looks at her drawing with a more curious look.

Counselor: "May I?" (Counselor motions to hold up drawing)

Melissa nods and slides her drawing across the table to be closer to the counselor.

Counselor: Sometimes we can notice things about our art, and even ourselves, once we step back and take a look at the art when we're finished. Does anything stand out to you in your drawing?

Melissa nods then points to the part of the drawing where she had used a lot of pink. She gave a little smile.

Counselor: Oh I see. Your favorite color.

Melissa smiles.

Counselor: In our future sessions together, we'll continue to do different types of art to learn more about each other and how your time here can be beneficial.

Melissa nods.

Counselor: It's up to you what you'd like to do with your art. You can take it with you or if you want I can hold onto it for you in a safe place.

Melissa: I'll take it.

Counselor: Would you like an envelope to place your drawing in? That way the oil pastels won't smear.

Melissa: (Nods her head yes)

As seen here, often during the first session, the student will choose me to start sharing my art first. By doing so, I can show her how art can be shared in an easy, simple, safe way. I then have the chance to role model and thank the student for listening and for their interest, emphasizing their ability to focus, listen intently, and demonstrate willingness to learn about another person. I then ask them if they would like to share, demonstrating genuine interest in their art, and in turn, who they are as an individual. This is where the focus shifts entirely to the student as the school counselor seeks understanding.

You'll also notice that there was no push for meaning of Melissa's drawing, as I knew that having her open up verbally would take some time. Instead, I aimed to help her see parts of herself in her art, setting the path for self-awareness. As you see in this session, the student did not speak much, but she did create art as a form of expression. As time went on, Melissa started to open up more about her art in the sessions with me. She described her art in more detail, rather than the initial shrugging or short 2- or 3-word responses. In the second half of the year, she was referred to a small group to further enhance her social and communication skills.

5.8 Art Processing and Counseling Theory

Processing student art in individual counseling can also depend on theoretical orientation. As discussed in Chapter 4, school counselors can choose to give art directives based on their chosen counseling theory, and therefore, the processing of the art would be grounded in the same way. In this section, as we have looked at how the processing of student art can look in different settings, I believe it is valuable to illustrate how to process student art through different theoretical orientations, too.

5.9 Solution-Focused Brief Therapy (SFBT) and Art Processing

In processing the "Bridge to a Miracle" Drawing described in Chapter 4, students are invited to share their desired outcome, or miracle, where all their problems are resolved as created in their art. A key component in this drawing is the student. From there, I can use the drawing to reference what they would be doing if their miracle was answered, and discuss if this could come into existence upon entering back into the classroom or other school setting from our session. This can spark thinking in their minds, as seen in the next case study.

Case Study: That Teacher Doesn't Like Me

In my time as a high school counselor, often I would have students come to my office asking if they could change their daily schedule of classes. Upon asking for the reason to change classes, some students were more forthright than others, stating they wanted to be in a class with their friend, or that they didn't like their teacher and wanted a different one who was "less strict." When I explained that not liking a teacher wasn't enough to warrant a schedule change, the narrative turned into, "Well, that teacher doesn't like me."

Once I had a student named Crystal with whom I had a good rapport. She would often drop by my office during lunch to vent about how much homework she had, or how annoying the staff were when attempting to clear the hallways and tell everyone to "Get to class!"

"I'm always on time Ms. Arroyo, but sometimes my class is on the other side of the building and they yellin' like I don't know I have to get to class."

"Well I'm glad to hear that you are able to get to class on time despite the distance. And sounds like you know the value of being on time too."

"It's just annoying. Anyway, I need to change my science class."

"Why is that?" I responded.

"That teacher doesn't like me, "Crystal affirmed.

"How do you know that the teacher doesn't like you?" I inquired.

"She's always yellin' at me. I do my work, I don't see what the problem is," she exclaimed.

"I'm going to need a little more information than that," I explained. I then said, "Let's take a look at this more closely. I want to help you, but I need to know if changing your class would be the best solution to the problem."

I then guided Crystal through all of the steps in the "Bridge to a Miracle," Drawing. Once she was finished, I asked if we could first look at her "Miracle" part of the drawing.

She explained that she was in a new science class with the new teacher. She was seated toward the back of the class, as interpreted through a stick figure with the face demonstrating a large smile. I stated, "It looks like you are really happy here, what are you thinking?"

"I'm thinking that I'm happy the teacher doesn't bother me and I'm mindin' my own business."

I then pointed to the teacher who was writing at the board. I asked, "What do you think the teacher would be talking about in this drawing?" Crystal replied, "I don't know, biology stuff."

"Okay, well let's take a look at your drawing of where you're at right now." "I motioned for us to view the left side of her drawing." "I see in this drawing you are sitting in the front of the class." Crystal stated, "Yeah, I hate it."

"So you're unhappy sitting in front?"

"Yeah Ms. Sutter always yellin' at me."

"About anything specific?"

"To put my phone away, or stop talking, It's always something."

"Ok well, what did you write in your bridge part of your drawing? What solutions do you have to get from the current situation to a miracle?"

"Change my class."

"Ok well here's where we'll need to work together to come up with more than one solution."

"So you're not going to change my class?"

"I'm not so sure if that would get you where you want to be. I see the main difference in the two pictures is where you sit. That won't be guaranteed if you were to switch teachers."

"Ugh. Ms. Sutter just all in my business."

I pointed to her drawing. "Ok, what are you doing in here that would warrant her being in your business."

"Last time she said if I don't put my phone away she will take it."

I asked, "Were you on your phone?"

"Well I had to check a text from my mom."

"I understand. Does this happen often?"

"Well, yeah, she's been sick lately and my sisters and I have to stay with my aunt."

"Ahh, I see. I understand why you would be worried and want to check your texts to see if your mom is okay."

"Yeah, but Ms. Sutter is mean she don't understand anything."

"What makes you say that?"

Crystal remained silent.

"I wonder if one of the solutions under your bridge drawing could be that she knew about what was happening with your mom."

"That doesn't matter she yelled at me before my mom got sick."

I said, "Well, we need to try different things because I'm not able to change your class, as the same thing may happen with your new teacher, who is most likely going to have the same expectation regarding phone use."

"I guess," she sighed and put her head down.

I said, "What do you think if somehow Ms. Sutter can have an idea of what is going on, how do you think she would change in this drawing of yours?"

"I don't know."

I said, "You can change it on your drawing."

She proceeded to scribble out the yelling marks coming from Ms. Sutter's mouth in her drawing.

The bell rang, and she got up and said, "Fine, I guess I can't change my class." I told her to stop by the following day.

She continued to stop by the next few days during lunch and updated me on her mom, who was going to come home from the hospital soon. She talked about how hard it was not knowing if she'd be ok and that she worried about her little sister, who was getting into trouble at school, most likely because she was missing her mom. She also shared that her sister started speaking with the counselor at her elementary school, which seemed to be helping.

I asked about Ms. Sutter, to which she said, "I'm not thinkin' about her I just mind my business and do my work." She also added that she didn't have her phone out as much, and it was on silent until the passing period, when she could check her texts. I acknowledged her choice to follow the class expectations regarding phone use, and how it must be difficult, especially since she worried about her family. She replied, "I guess Ms. Arroyo, I'll be alright!" and smiled. I encouraged her to continue making positive choices before she left for her next class.

In this case, Crystal didn't follow one of the solutions under her bridge nor the one I suggested. However, she found a solution that came about after talking about the stress of her mom not feeling well, and having to move in with her aunt temporarily. It seemed to solve the problem with her teacher regarding the cell phone policy as she chose to check texts during passing periods.

Sometimes the miracle world a student desires is the world in which they already are - they just needed to see it in their drawings, discover the details, and come up with attainable solutions to resolve the problem at hand.

5.10   Cognitive Behavioral Theory (CBT) and Art Processing

When integrating CBT into art therapy approaches, the art allows for a greater understanding of what the student feels in the moment, the thoughts that contribute to that feeling, and the impact on their actions. Often the feeling becomes overwhelming, and actions taken by the student result in negative outcomes. The work here is to have the student see this for themselves through their own art, giving a starting point to challenging irrational beliefs.

Let's take a look at how CBT with an art therapy approach in school counseling can help a student identify first the difference between a thought and a feeling, second, how a thought can impact how they feel, and third, how they can impact their actions and behaviors.

Case Study: Richard

Richard came to my office one day, which in recent weeks had become more often. His head was lowered and he appeared sad. It was the beginning of his senior year, which he had been looking forward to all last year as a junior. Unfortunately, his last year in high school was entirely different from what he had envisioned. In the second week of school, he was caught on school grounds with some friends after hours. As a result, he received an in-school suspension for one day. During this time, he found out that his girlfriend had been cheating on him with his friend the summer before. He ended up getting into a physical fight in the cafeteria with his friend over this. As a consequence, he received a three-day out-of-school suspension, was removed from the football team, and was not allowed to attend the Homecoming dance. Prior to these events, Richard shared with me that he had a complicated relationship with his mother and no longer talked to her. He moved in with his father the previous year. All of this took a toll on him, and a few weeks before he expressed having suicidal ideation. After gathering more information, I started a support plan with him and his father to keep him safe. His father also followed through on a referral to therapy services outside school, which Richard began soon after.

That day Richard came into my office he sat down and his eyes started to well with tears.

"It looks like you're having a rough start to the day," I said.

He nodded his head. He grabbed a tissue and put his head in his hands.

I said, "Take your time."

When he was done wiping his tears, I asked, "What are your tears saying?"

He stated, "Like my senior year is ruined."

I responded, "I can understand how you could feel like this way, however, your senior year is not over yet."

He stated, "I just feel like I can't trust anyone."

I said, "Well, let's take a look at that statement. It's a thought that you are having, that you can't trust anyone, that's not a feeling."

He said, "Well, whatever it is, it's the truth."

I said, "Ok, why don't we do this?" I pointed to the paper and opened up the box of oil pastels at the table we were sitting at. I said,

> *What I would like you to do is draw out how you are feeling right now. It can look any way you'd like to, you can choose any color, draw lines, shapes, whatever you think looks like how you feel right now.*

He sat up slowly, then chose his paper and started looking at the oil pastels. Once he got started on his drawing, I let him know that I needed to call the college and career center to let them know I'd be late to the meeting held there, but that he did not have to rush.

Once I made my call, I turned on classical music for background sound. After about seven minutes or so, he finished his drawing and wiped his hands of the oil pastel marks with baby wipes that were on the table.

I asked if I could take a look at his drawing, and he nodded, and I turned it so we could both look at it. He used black construction paper on which he created a big black circle in the middle, with blue and white circles blended together around, reaching the edges of the paper.

I asked, "Could you walk me through what you created?"

He said, "The black circle is the hole I can't get out of."

I stated, "I see. The black circle also takes up a lot of space on the paper. Was that intentional?"

He agreed, stating, "Yeah, I feel like that every day."

I said, "Do you feel that way, or do you think that way?"

He looked confused and I said, "Well, feeling like you are in a black hole is not the feeling, it's the thought. How does the thought of being in a black hole make you feel?"

He stated, "Depressed."

You must have this thought a lot. He stated, "Yeah," as he looked at the picture, and said, "That's why that black circle is so big."

I asked, "What does the blue and white stand for?"

He said that those colors were his favorite color combination. I said, "That makes sense, your gym shoes are blue and white." They appeared brand new, and he looked down at them and said, "Yeah." He explained that his dad got them for him as part of his back-to-school gear.

"So, the blue and white in this picture represent something positive," I asked for clarity.

"I guess."

I said, "Well, I notice your drawing isn't entirely black, the blue and white combination surrounds it."

He remained quiet. I stated,

I mention this because I remember not too long ago that you said your dad has been supportive of you this past year, even though he wasn't happy at all with the events of the beginning of this school year. But he acknowledges that you've had a rough go, and that it doesn't define who you are. At least that's the sentiment I get when I've spoken to him and how you've described him.

He nodded.

So, I say this to say that your thought of not being able to get out of the black hole is not entirely true. Thoughts aren't always facts. Your dad supports you, you can come seek me out when you need help like you did today.

I asked if he could think of anyone else that he trusts, and he mentioned the assistant football coach, his older brother, and his best friend at school.

"So if you're in a hole so to speak, you have people who support you and can help you."

He nodded.

I said, "So, if you think instead, 'I can get out of this black hole, and there are people who can help me. And I've gotten through tough situations before', how would that make you feel?"

He said, "Better."

"Maybe, this thought has more truth to it?"

He stated, "Yeah."

I said, "Well, sounds like you can start practicing having that thought instead. I recommend looking at your shoes with your favorite color combination as a reminder."

He gave a half smile.

I asked if he felt ready to go back to class, to which he agreed, and I informed that he can check in with me again as he needed to in the upcoming days. I asked if he wanted his drawing or if he would like me to hold on to it. He chose the latter.

Richard eventually joined club sports mid-school year to keep himself active. Throughout the year, I remarked that his grades were solid and considering all that he had been through, he maintained his grade point average above a 3.2. He also improved on his college admission test the second time he took it. He eventually applied and was accepted into a two-year college on a full scholarship, with plans to transfer to a university afterward.

In the above example, you will see that using art helped Richard to create on paper the negative thoughts that consumed his mind. When pointing out that he had colors on his drawing that represented something positive, it helped to shift his way of thinking. Encouraging him to practice thoughts that were aligned with the truth was facilitated using his art.

5.11 Person-Centered Theory and Art Processing

In my experience, Person-Centered Therapy (PCT) is effective to use when a student may not have the ability to come up with solutions, or even be able to identify a problem, as would happen in Solution-Focused theory. Alternatively, they may not be at a place where they are able to understand cause and effect, or may not be able to identify thoughts that affect feelings and actions, strategies used in CBT. Instead, the student may simply need to be heard, and have their thoughts and feelings validated before they can develop the skills to make more positive choices.

While supporting a student in processing their artwork using Person-Centered Theory, it is important to acknowledge the student's participation, as well as listening and responding to what the student shares through their art verbally or through their facial expressions and body language. Reflecting back to the student what they have communicated through their art, allows for processing the art while demonstrating empathy, a core tenet of PCT (Yao & Kabir, 2023).

Case Study: Jeanette

One day the security guard peeked into my office and asked if I had some time to meet with Jeanette, who was upset and not ready to return to class from recess. I agreed as I knew she needed additional support in times of distress. Jeanette typically would see the social worker on days like this, as she received counseling services per her Individual Education Plan (IEP) for Specialized Services. However, on this day, the social worker was working at her other assigned school, so Jeanette was entrusted with me.

Jeanette and her sister, who was also in seventh grade, were known to be involved in any type of conflict or physical fight amongst the girls in the same grade. On that day, she presented as quiet, but not in a timid way. At first glance, it appeared that she was analyzing whether or not she could trust me. I was aware that she was limited in her verbal communication skills, and was in a classroom with other students who also received special education services that was separate from other seventh grade students in the general education classroom.

I asked her to have a seat at the table, where I typically have pencils, markers, multimedia paper, and stickers readily available.

"It sounds like you need some time before returning to class."

She looked at me, then looked away, nodding her head yes. As she didn't usually come to see me, I informed her about my process of speaking with students to help them, and about confidentiality, just as her social worker had already established with her in her sessions. She didn't say anything.

I followed with, "Did something in particular happen at recess that was upsetting?" She nodded looking around my room. "Would you be willing to share what happened so that I can help you feel less upset?" She shrugged her shoulders.

Next, I told her that she could draw out what happened at recess rather than having to talk about the events. I informed her that being able to see what happened, helps me to understand the situation better. She appeared to be open to it, so I asked her to choose her paper out of the various sizes I had on the table, and moved the markers and pencils closer to her. I explained that she could use stick figures if she'd like, and that I wouldn't be grading her art. She proceeded to draw as I observed, getting right to work without any hesitation.

Once she stopped drawing, I asked her, "Are you finished?" She nodded and crossed her arms. After this, I asked if I could take a look at it, and she nodded. I asked her if I could move her artwork so we could both have a better view, and with her permission, I angled the picture so we could both see clearly. You can see Jeanette's drawing in Figure 5.3.

When I looked at her drawing, I informed Jeanette that a couple of things stood out to me and asked her if she could tell me more about them. When I pointed to the left side of the picture, she explained that one of the figures was herself, and the other figure was the person with whom she almost had a fight during recess. The figure of her had a smile on her face. I told her that she appears to be happy there, and I asked her if that was the case. She nodded yes. I also pointed to all the stick figures surrounding her and the other student that were in the formation of a circle. She stated that those were all the students who

Figure 5.3 Jeanette's drawing of what happened at recess.

were watching them about to fight. I asked if that was what made her happy, and she nodded yes.

I also asked her to tell me more about another part of her drawing, the upper right side of her drawing, as seen in Figure 5.3. She stated that it was her again, and the other student. I pointed out to her that in this close-up picture of the two of them, she appeared scared. She looked at the picture of herself, where she drew her facial expression with her mouth frowning and eyebrows positioned in a way that made her appear nervous. A few seconds went by before Jeanette nodded her head yes. I pointed out the difference between how she appeared to feel in the two parts of the drawing. When asked what happened after the scene she drew out, she let me know that was when the teachers and security guard became involved before any fighting started, and then she was taken to my office.

In an effort process Jeanette's art using unconditional positive regard approach in PCT, I mirrored back what she represented in her drawing to validate her feelings without judgement. I let her know that it is understandable to be happy when she has attention, especially from her peers. I also let her know that it is understandable to feel scared at the same time. I said, "In a fight you can get hurt, so it's understandable to be afraid." She nodded, and I affirmed for her that it was okay to have different feelings and thoughts about situations, and that she can learn to make decisions that are best for her, keeping her safe and happy. She nodded again. Before the session ended, I asked if it was okay if I shared what was discussed in our session with her social worker, so that she could continue to process what happened the next time she met with her.

In the case with Jeanette, she was not in a place where she could identify a problem, let alone a solution, as typically used with SFBT, or come up with thoughts behind feelings, such as with CBT. Therefore, using person-centered techniques to process her art, though with little words, helped her begin to accept and gain greater awareness of her actions. She was able to demonstrate and receive empathy, and she began to understand that she became involved in fighting and conflict because of the attention she received, even if she also was scared. Although there wasn't a definitive solution at the end of the session, it was also a way for me as the school counselor to advocate for strong Tier 1 Universal programming to promote social/emotional learning development, and reinforcement of school-wide expectations, such as Be Respectful, Be Responsible, and Be Safe, in all school settings, in particular the playground when fights tended to occur. This is especially important during the adolescent years, when students thrive on acceptance from their peers while they are also developing who they are as a person. Instead of students like Jeanette obtaining attention from fighting, students can learn healthier behaviors, develop effective coping skills, the ability to resolve conflict, and the ability to communicate their needs in all settings. which all align to the ASCA Student Mindset and Behavior Standards.

5.12 Conclusion

In this chapter, we explored the "art" of processing student art. Being able to process art helps to gain a deeper understanding of the student and their situations, thoughts, feelings, and experiences, all in a piece of art that was made in 20 minutes or less. The best interpretation of the art is from the student who created it, so the task of the school counselor is to be able to facilitate this for the student. Considerations to process art in the classroom, small group, and in individual counseling were discussed to maximize the potential that art has for healing, learning, and growth. Processing the art in relation to theoretical orientation was also discussed, using the art to enhance the practice, and bringing forth the objectives of our counseling practice in a way that may not have been done as quickly through only verbal communication. Finally, treating the art in the way we would treat the student, with respect and care, to foster trust among peers if the art is processed as a group, as well as with the counselor, can help the student to use the art to become more aware of themselves and others, develop valuable skills, setting them up to be successful in school and in life.

References

American School Counselor Assciation. (2021). *ASCA student standards; Mindsets and behaviors for student success*. Author.

Britannica, T. Editors of Encyclopaedia (2024, November 14). Inferiority Complex. Encyclopedia Britannica. https://www.britannica.com/science/inferiority-complex

Cedeno, R., Torrico, T. J. Adlerian Therapy. [Updated 2024 Jan 11]. In: StatPearls [Internet]. Treasure Island (FL): StatPearls Publishing; 2024 Jan-. Available from: https://www.ncbi.nlm.nih.gov/books/NBK599518/

Wright, R. J. (2011). *Introduction to school counseling*. Sage Publications, Inc.

Yao, L., & Kabir, R. Person-Centered Therapy (Rogerian Therapy) [Updated 2023 Feb 9]. In: StatPearls [Internet]. Treasure Island (FL): StatPearls Publishing; 2025 Jan-. Available from: https://www.ncbi.nlm.nih.gov/books/NBK589708/

Chapter 6

Art for School Counselors

Integrating Art Therapy Approaches
in Professional Development

Throughout this book, we've talked about how students can benefit from art therapy approaches within school counseling practices, supporting them in learning critical student standards for success in school, college, career, and beyond. However, as mentioned in Chapter 1, these art therapy approaches provide benefits to adults as well. The work of a school counselor can be overwhelming and exhausting, with high caseloads, high expectations, and few resources in the school community to match. This, along with other factors, has led to discontentment and many highly trained professionals leaving the field.

In this final chapter, we will look deeper into how learning about art therapy to use with students can simultaneously support school counselors, and, in turn, help to retain school counselors in the profession. As school counselors become trained in using art to benefit their students, they can use these skills to benefit from their own creative process, allowing time for reflection and growth within themselves. First, let's take a look at the field of school counseling and the challenge we are facing as a profession.

6.1 Where Are the School Counselors?

In the past several years, there has been a shortage of educators nationwide. According to the National Center for Education Statistics, 86% of K-12 public schools reported challenges hiring teachers for the 2023–2024 school year, with 83% reporting trouble hiring for non-teacher positions, such as the "mental health professional" roles (National Assessment of Educational Progress, 2023), which include school counselor positions. Reasons for school counselor shortage were present before the pandemic – burnout from high caseloads intensified by high levels of need, multiple crises at a time, inappropriate duties such as test coordination and records maintenance, and serving as a substitute teacher or as a "social-emotional" teacher in the master schedule are just some of the reasons I've heard school counselors express are the reasons for feeling frustrated and unhappy. Though the purpose of being placed in these non-counseling positions was to fill the shortages in other spaces, it still didn't stop the sense of

DOI: 10.4324/9781003430940-9

frustration. Having the education, training, and background to help students in a meaningful way, and not being able to fully apply them, then being blamed by team members for not providing enough for students, leads to disheartenment, and ultimately, many leaving the field altogether.

School counselors are considered mental-health-based professionals in their communities, and the shortage causes inequitable access to valuable services that can help students succeed in school, college, and their future careers, all of which contribute positively to their lives beyond high school. More than 70% of children receive mental health support in a school-based setting (Francies & Silva-Padron, 2024). As we know, the mental health needs of students were evident before the pandemic and were gravely impacted by it, which led to effects in the years following, all impacting their ability to learn. Nevertheless, school counselors were expected to take the lead in addressing these challenges, while also having to address their own recovery from the pandemic. So, what can be done?

Addressing the shortage involves a multifaceted approach, including increasing funding for schools, leading to hiring more counselors to reduce the school counselor-to-student ratio, and offering competitive salaries to make work-life balance attainable, which are a few first critical steps (American School Counselor Association, 2023). However, these strategies will take some time, as advocacy for funding public education overall has been a process for many years.

Another more accessible strategy to retain school counselors is to provide professional development that is applicable and effective to the diverse and evolving needs of the students they serve (Hooker, 2022) (Francies & Silva-Padron, 2024). In this chapter, I will discuss my experience as a school counseling specialist in the district where I started weaving art therapy approaches into professional development, discovering that school counselors can find moments of self-care and connection with others. By doing so, it provided a means, albeit briefly, to encompass one of the ASCA Ethical Standards of School Counselors: B.3.h. Recognize the potential for stress and secondary trauma and practice wellness and self-care through monitoring mental, emotional, and physical health, while seeking consultation from an experienced school counseling practitioner and or others as needed (American School Counselor Association, 2022).

6.2   Integrating Art Therapy Approaches in Professional Development

When I started my position as a specialist, it was in the summer of 2020, right at the height of the pandemic. No longer in the building to address the needs of students, I was now addressing the needs of school counselors. The unprecedented nature of the pandemic led to a call to action from our department to help school counselors be equipped with training, resources, and tools to alleviate the stress of students, families, and the communities at large. During my first year as a specialist providing professional development for a large urban district, I quickly learned that when training lacks meaning and is only focused on outcomes, school counselors make their dissatisfaction clear. This feedback comes in various forms: direct comments, disengaged body language, uninterested expressions, few questions – or, at the other extreme, a slew of questions about how the material connects to their daily challenges, or how it can be implemented at all.

I came across many novice mistakes in my approach, and as time went on, I learned the ins and outs of providing impactful professional development. What I came to discover firsthand is the definition of *meaningful* professional development – training that not only directly addresses what counselors do daily, but one that creates a space for reflection, self-care, and a sense of community among counselors facing similar challenges. After all, school counselors are busy professionals with a lot on their plates, and any time spent outside of their school building should be deemed valuable and necessary. As Aguilar and Cohen (2022) state,

> For professional development to be a transformative process, learners are actively engaged, and for which the aim is to explore and expand behaviors, beliefs, and ways of being; a learning process that results in a change of practice. It is a process to cultivate self-awareness and understanding, social awareness and understanding, community development, and individual and collective empowerment.
>
> (Aguilar & Cohen, 2022)

During a professional learning committee meeting, after making my usual district announcements and updates pertinent to school counselors, I decided to share one art directive for school counselors to use when working with students to help them identify different emotions. As papers and markers were passed out, the hesitancy and reluctance to participate became apparent. I'd hear among the participants, "Oh no, I cannot draw at all, I'm a terrible artist," or, "I'm not creative." To that, I'd respond, "Now what would you say to your students if you heard them pass such hard judgment on themselves?" I'd get a bit of relaxation and laughter on their part, getting their buy-in to be present and non-judgmental as they embark on the creative process.

From then I recognized the importance of setting up a safe space for school counselors in a professional development setting, just as I would with students. Understandably, anyone in education may feel "not good enough," as the sense of not accomplishing enough during the school day due to the high caseloads and expectations from administration, and the little time to meet them all. So, when school counselors are out of the building to receive training, it's important to set up a space where they don't feel they will be judged for not getting an intervention up quickly enough, or not having enough time to prepare for an upcoming college or career event, or to be able to check on all the students who need a follow-up from being hospitalized immediately upon their return to school, or to make sure all of the new students are transitioning well, or having all the students complete their college and financial aid applications, or making sure scheduling classes for students are done in a timely manner. The to-do list goes on and on.

6.3   Setting the Space to Spark Creativity

I distinctly remember one school counselor, upon placing a sticker in the middle of her paper, holding her head in her hands as she stared down at her paper. I walked over to them and recommended to pick a color or two, and if they'd like, they can simply fill the space with those colors, create lines, symbols, or designs; the choice was up to them. I reminded them of there being no expectation to have their art look like anything specific.

One helpful reminder that I use to ease participation in the art-making process is to say,

> *If anyone is creative it's you all! Having worked in a public school where the needs are high and resources are few, I'm willing to bet you've had to be creative in order to meet the needs of your students and families.*

I then let them know that artistic skills and abilities per se are not the goal of making art. I ask them to express themselves in a way that will be unique to each of them. Just as I would recommend to students, I instruct school counselors that if any judgmental thought comes up, place it on a cloud and let it float away. School counselors are able to relate to that guidance, since this is what they do to build self-awareness and confidence for their own students. Now, they can benefit from what they teach their students.

Participating in creative activities to possess the qualities we want to instill in our students enhances our practice. We can serve as role models as we embrace our whole selves, including liberating our thoughts, ideas, feelings through art. With the opportunity to reignite creativity among the school counselors for themselves, ideas start to flow.

During a discussion in another training, school counselors suddenly started sharing ideas of their own art directives that were valuable in their practice. It was sort of a popcorn effect, where one counselor shared an idea, then immediately another, and so on. One counselor shared that the emoji sticker drawing can be a form of data collection – having the student create a drawing on how they felt before a session and how they felt after the session, making a two-sided drawing, as a quick and efficient way to gain pre- and post-results to see if the school counseling service had an impact. Another school counselor encouraged using cost-effective mini canvases with mini easels they discovered at a local store, for students to paint freely whenever they are in distress. Yet, another school counselor shared that they have an accordion-style art journal with 8–10 pages for their students, to create a page every time they are in a session with the counselor. He described it as an easy and efficient way for both school counselor and student to monitor weekly their progress toward goals in short-term counseling. When creativity flows and ideas are shared, school counselors implement new and innovative ways to enhance their practice, and the students benefit as a result.

6.4 Creativity and School Counselor Strengths

During a meeting with school counselors, facilitated the "Animal for a Day," art directive during a Professional Learning Community for school counselors. Some counselors were more excited than others to participate, with the latter commenting on their lack of artistic technical skills, despite the setup of a non-judgmental environment. Once the clay was passed out, you can see counselors immediately working with the clay and talking with each other about what they were going to create. Once they completed their animals, I directed them to share them with a partner and process their experiences. When I brought the group of counselors back together as a large group, they talked about how they enjoyed hearing about their colleagues' animals, in particular the strengths they highlighted. When asked how they could identify with their animals, one school counselor shared that she wanted to be a kangaroo for a day, because they have the strength and the pouch to carry all they need to go about their day. See Figure 6.1.Before this counselor left the meeting, she showcased all the bags she carried to work every day, from her lunch bag, to her computer bag, to a supply bag, to her purse. Much like the kangaroo, the school counselor carried the resources she needed to help her get through a busy, yet productive day.

Providing the opportunity to participate and experiment in creative activities in professional development while connecting with peers, gives time to pause and reflect, welcoming in new ideas and receiving the encouragement to implement them in their practice upon returning to school. Experiencing the benefits of creativity

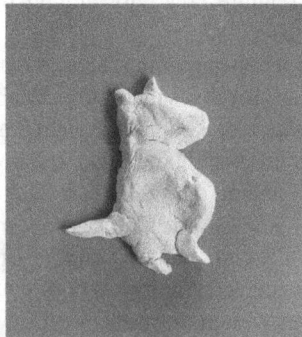

Figure 6.1 A school counselor's "Animal for the Day" is a kangaroo.

firsthand can be motivating and can start to show up in all aspects of school counseling services. As a result, students embrace these same benefits – pausing, reflecting, connecting, and overall feeling inspired through their own creativity and art.

Let's ART About This

Recognizing what made art-making so beneficial, I decided that it was time to bring that back in my new role. The purpose became twofold: (1) School counselors would learn a strategy to utilize with their students immediately and (2) School counselors would have a safe space to experience the benefits of art-making strategies for themselves.

All the benefits of art therapy describe what makes professional development a transformative process: actively engaged learners as they explore and expand behaviors, beliefs, and ways of being, develop social and self-awareness and understanding, a sense of community, and individual and collective empowerment (Aguilar & Cohen, 2022). After seeing results, I became intentional about infusing art within professional development whenever and wherever I had the chance. It became much like meeting the objectives in the training as it would in a classroom lesson with students. This time, my goal was to ensure that ASCA professional standards were addressed in the process. Just as I integrated art therapy approaches in school counseling to enhance my practice, I approached my role as a school counseling specialist in a similar way. Whether it was presenting at a School Counselor Leadership Meeting, in a Professional Learning Committee of School Counselors, or training on adolescent development in college and career advising, I took what was already part of my role and made intentional space for art-making. A norm was for participants to allow themselves the luxury of doing one thing. To close their laptops, put phones to the side, be fully present, and participate in art. Any worries of whether they had time to eat their lunch that day, or if someone from the office needed them immediately, were to be placed on a cloud. This time was for them. Though I am unable to change the landscape of the school counseling field, having art to at least momentarily reduce the stress from work appears to be all that is needed in the moment.

6.5   Responding to National and Local Crises with an Art Therapy Approach

Shortly after the tragic shooting of elementary school students and teachers in Uvalde, Texas, I was asked to develop and facilitate professional development training for school counselors when responding to a national and local crisis to address the social and emotional needs of the school community. At the district level, we knew how important it was to equip school counselors to support their school communities when national tragedies occur, as well as offer training in the event that fatalities happen on a local level.

Fortunately, crises to this extent do not happen in a school community frequently to on an hourly or daily basis. However, they do happen and are anticipated enough that the need for specific training on this topic was warranted. The uptick in national and local news of school shootings leading to fatalities needed to be addressed with the sensitivity and care of students who may be triggered by these events or closely affiliated with them. School counselors need to prepare and be equipped to be as effective as they can be should the time come.

In one part of the training, I introduced an activity intended to assist individual students or small groups who may need intensive support after a crisis. The participants were made aware of the rationale of the use of art, which was to create mini-drawings to contain strong emotions as a result of varying levels of crisis. After the stage was set up for making art in a safe and inclusive space, the school counselors started drawing, and in little time appeared relaxed yet focused intently on their art. The room became quiet, as much of the sounds of chatter slowly faded away. School counselors are actively engaged in making marks on their paper, and the only sounds you can hear are the caps of markers coming on and off, or pencils being placed down on the table for another color to be picked up. (See Figure 6.2).

Figure 6.2 A school counselor creates around their emoji stickers.

When everyone received the prompt to share their art with a partner, a shift in the room took place as the energy of curiosity of others' artwork and experiences filled the space. The sharing of art among the school counselors and the conversations that arose were none like I've seen in other professional development sessions I've provided before. It was as though walls that were built around each school counselor all came down once they started sharing their art with one another. Discussions can be heard about the difficult work at hand when it came to responding to crises, especially when going through a multitude of their own thoughts and emotions. There seemed to be a buiding of community in the room as they shared with one another, and in all took less than 20 minutes of time. I remember one school counselor shared that she didn't realize how much of an impact living in a city for a year had on becoming a school counselor. Coming from out of state and growing up in a suburb, she quickly realized through reflecting on her art, the vastly different experience she had growing up compared to her students. In her drawing she included scenes of her hometown, the people, and her old school. She acknowledged how much more she needed to know about her students' backgrounds and experiences in order to grow as a school counselor and address the needs of her students effectively during a crisis.

Figure 6.3 School counselors share and process their art with one another.

Another shared what their whole morning looked like prior to walking into the training. It was a struggle in comparison to other days, after dropping off the kids - the rain, traffic, and not knowing where to park - had caused added stress, which they reflected in their mini-drawing. This led to a discussion of how many school counselors have to balance all of their responsibilities in and outside of work. They all began to encourage, help, and listen to one another, sparking a sense of relief and joy to be among others who listened and understood. (See Figure 6.3). This moment of self-awareness and compassion for themselves and others sparked by the art was used to highlight the importance of self-care, attending to their needs, and connecting with others. As they do so, they are in a better place to help school communities through a national or local crisis.

6.6 Pilot Study: School Counselors Integrating Art Therapy Approaches

It's easy to become jaded after working in public education in a large urban district. Obtaining funding to support programs, resources, and initiatives seem elusive. But, sometimes the requests are answered. One year our district received a grant to address the mental health of students as well as the school counselor shortage. At around this time, school counselors voiced their concerns to our department about the need for more training on interventions to address mental health issues, such as the increased referrals for anxiety, as well as the unprecedented increase in enrollment of newcomer students, to which they wanted to ensure their specific needs are met, as mentioned in Chapter 2.

Upon the success of larger-scale professional development demonstrating the use of art therapy directives, I proposed the idea of training school counselors in integrating art therapy approaches to fulfill both intentions of the grant. Additionally, up until this point, I had come upon little research on the integration of art therapy in school counseling. It provided an opportunity to study closely whether or not the approaches I've been using in the course of my career can be translated through training other school counselors, therefore reaching diverse student populations, while analyzing the qualitative and quantitative impact. That's where a pilot group studying the impact of art therapy integrated into school counseling was born and is still in the process today. What I will highlight for the purpose of this chapter is how the art serves to validate the work school counselors do and the impact it has on students.

I was able to recruit eight school counselors interested in learning more about art therapy, as the majority of them had already been implementing art-making with students. They learned the foundation of art therapy, participated in the art directives, and received training on how to facilitate each art directive to maximize the art-making process and art piece for the students they planned to work with in a small group. As part of the pilot, the school counselors were to implement nine small group, art therapy-integrated, counseling sessions to students who were referred for a Tier II Intervention, where learning the mindset and behaviors of effective coping skills and a sense of belonging would be addressed to close any gap in academic achievement or discipline referrals.

Midway through the pilot, school counselors in the cohort came together for a community of practice, where each school counselor could share a problem of practice or student artwork to discuss its impact on student progress. One school counselor was implementing the group with middle school self-identifying male students, referred for disruptive behavior in the classroom and other settings. She shared her experience thus far, which she described was a stark contrast to her first implementation of the small group in the previous semester, where she provided the sessions to a small group of Kindergarten and first grade students. She described that work as rewarding, remarking on how the students focused on their art, enjoyed the process, and bonded with each other during each session they created and shared their art. The group with the middle school boys was not as smooth, warm, and fuzzy as this previous group, and she expressed concern that the group and the art-making process were not making any impact. She shared that the boys spent the majority of the time in sessions "one-upping" each other, egging each other on, or getting out of their seats. The school counselor provided frequent redirection to the task at hand. She described their art as minimal compared to her previous group with the younger students. However, when we looked at the student art as part of the community of practice, it seemed to appear otherwise.

Describing one student's art, the school counselor facilitating the boys' group explained that he based it on an inspirational sticker, with the quote, "You're Awesome." He shared with the school counselor and the group that he had become used to others telling him he is always doing something wrong, making it hard to believe when someone complimented him. He added that he didn't trust those who complimented him were telling the truth. At the same time, he recognized the value in receiving positive comments and believing in them, so he could feel better about himself. As a result, he chose this sticker and drew around it to create an inspirational art piece that reminded him that he is, in fact, awesome. See Figure 6.4.

The school counselors in the group commented on this student's art, along with the other boys' art in the group, pointing out their ability to participate and create meaningful art. They further noted that the art served as a visible representation of the boys' reflection of their own patterns of thinking and how it negatively affected them. Finally, it served as evidence that they were able to come up with the solution, through their art, to correct unhelpful thoughts, and believe thoughts that help them make better choices for themselves.

In this example of professional development, proof of effective practice is in the art. Its visual and tangible nature is hard to deny, playing a part in helping both school counselor and student of the learning and growth obtained. As long as we are open to exploring creativity, the possibilities are endless. Art reveals not just the inner workings of students, but the impact school counselors make on students, providing opportunities to learn skills that set them up for success in school and in life.

Figure 6.4 A sixth-grade student's art to remind themselves of their value.

6.7   Conclusion

Although I was no longer working directly with students, training school counselors in art therapy approaches allows for more students to access the benefits. It feels like a shared mission, knowing that my support contributes to the vital work counselors are doing every day in schools. The work isn't done yet, and as described in this chapter, when school counselors are equipped with the tools and training in a supportive environment, they can recognize what they already have within. We need to create more of these opportunities. In the next and final chapter, we will discuss how we can make this happen, and continue this work.

References

Aguilar, E., & Cohen, L. (2022). *The PD book: 7 Habits that transform professional development*. John Wiley & Sons, Inc.

American School Counselor Association. (2022). *ASCA ethical standards for school counselors*. American School Counselor Association. https://www.schoolcounselor. org/getmedia/44f30280-ffe8-4b41-9ad8-f15909c3d164/EthicalStandards.pdf

American School Counselor Association. (2023, September). *School counselor shortages*. Current Issues in Education. American School Counselor Association. https://www.schoolcounselor.org/getmedia/f73304ab-5ac5-4ba5-8342-826a3bc205a2/CIE-Employment-Shortages.pdf

Francies, C., & Silva-Padron, G. (2024, January 25). *Recruiting and retaining school-based mental health professionals*. Education Commission of the States. https://www.ecs.org/recruiting-and-retaining-school-based-mental-health-professionals/

Hooker, C. (2022, November 15). How to recruit and retain school counselors in your district. Hooked on Innovation. https://hookedoninnovation.com/2022/11/02/how-to-recruit-and-retain-school-counselors-in-your-district/

National Assessment of Educational Progress. (2023, October 17). Most public schools face challenges in hiring teachers and other personnel entering the 2023–24 academic year [Press Release]. https://nces.ed.gov/whatsnew/press_releases/10_17_2023.asp#:~:text=spp/results.asp-,Key%20Findings,teaching%20positions%20(76%20percent)

Conclusion

As we come to a close, I hope that you have been inspired to start integrating art therapy approaches into your work as a school counselor. This book can serve as a reference, with the first part serving as a resource to advocate for using art in your practice. Chapter 1 provides the foundation of art therapy, including key founders and research over the years demonstrating its impact, helping to connect the history and development of the field to the work of a school counselor.

The integration of art therapy aligns with both the ASCA Ethical Standards, as highlighted in Chapter 2, specifically when it comes to practicing with an equity lens. Keeping that at the forefront of our work helps to reach all students by providing services based on their specific needs. The ability of art therapy approaches to be culturally responsive and trauma-informed, is vital to working with historically under-resourced populations, makes it even more reason to embrace the integration in our practice to meet the needs of increasingly diverse student populations.

To round out Part I of the book, Chapter 3 discusses how integrating art therapy aligns with teaching students the ASCA Student Standards, or the mindsets and behaviors found by research to attribute to college and career success. Student art can facilitate the learning of these core standards in all three domains: career, social emotional, and academic, in a way that is tangible and visible, increasing students' confidence, belief in themselves, and sense of belonging in school, opening up a world of possibilities that students may not have discovered otherwise.

Part II of this book provided guidance on where to begin facilitating art therapy approaches. Chapter 4 covered what's needed, the considerations for art medium and materials, and art directives as they relate to counseling theory. What's important to remember from this chapter is that much can be created with even the simplest materials and directives. Moreover, you may find yourself coming up with art directives as you learn more about your students and as ideas come to mind to help them reach their goals. Chapter 5 walks through what to do now that the art has been created. Intentional processing of the art within the role of the school counselor can be transformative, as students gain a deeper understanding of themselves through their art. A key takeaway from this chapter is that the student is the only interpreter of their art, and school counselors are there to help them discover the significance of their creations. From there, the school counselor is aware of the next steps students can take to be on a successful path in school and in their future.

Chapter 6, the final chapter, showcases the possibilities of art for school counselors and their well-being. As school counselors create their own art to learn about art therapy and how they can use approaches with their students, they learn more about themselves than expected. Being in-tuned with ourselves as practitioners only enhances practice, as it helps to be in-tuned with our students and what they need. The art created among school counselors also develops a connection, allowing for community while gaining valuable professional development. When school counselors feel equipped and there are opportunities to fulfill their self-care, even for a brief moment, it helps to sustain a valuable profession that supports our youth as they navigate their journeys to high school graduation and beyond.

C.1   Future Direction in Research and Practice

Though I recognize that the experiences I've shared were based in Chicago, I truly believe that the universality of art and its benefits can be integrated into school counseling practice no matter the school community – public, private, small or large district, rural or urban. And, more importantly, there's a hunger for it.

A few years ago, when I was told that I'd have a banquet hall to present on this topic at the American School Counselor Association, I panicked. Will I have enough art materials? Will that many people even come? Why can't I just have a smaller room, where I can have a more intimate setting for the school counselors to create and process their art? After all the worry, the space was filled with over 300 school counselors. Once they engaged in the art-making part of the presentation, the noise level was significantly reduced to only the instrumental music in the background. School counselors from across the country were focused and invested in their art. When asked to share with a partner, the room became loud with eagerness to share about the art that was just created. This demonstrates the power of art and how engaging and rewarding it can be for both students and counselors alike.

Back in my school district, the desire to learn more about art therapy continues. At the time of writing this conclusion, I sent another call for 18 school counseling research participants for another cohort similar to the pilot cohort mentioned in Chapter 6. Over 150 applications came in after only a few days. In the applications, some school counselors shared their desire to be part of the research, as they've already seen the benefit with their students who struggle to communicate past trauma or worries verbally. And then there were others, who explained that even though their school had an art teacher, not all students in the building were able to have art class as part of their schedule. I've even had art teachers and social workers inquiring to be part of the research. The desire to integrate art as a therapeutic and healing modality in the learning environment of schools is evident.

It's clear that we need to continue research in integrating art therapy approaches not only in school counseling practice, but in all aspects of education. Students who go to a school where the arts are embraced in all aspects of the community should not be considered a luxury or a privilege, but the norm. And why end there? We can continue research on the integration of music, drama, and dance/movement therapy on the impact on academic achievement. Research may demonstrate benefits of the arts as integrated into the academic courses, offering a means to learning and growth through a different modality. We could discover the relationship of the arts integrated into the school day on a daily basis can lead to students feeling confident in themselves and what they have to contribute to the school setting and beyond.

C.2   My Overall Hope

Art allows us to flourish as human beings, helping us embrace our uniqueness, express our emotions, appreciate subjectivity, accept multiple truths, and be vulnerable in connecting with others. If students are able to create art in a safe space of their school, they can engage and create for pure enjoyment, rather than focusing on making it look aesthetically pleasing to others. In a world that values outcomes over process, this may be how we make a more productive society. Art can make us better, happier people for ourselves and the societies we live in. Educational systems nationwide need to shift the focus from immediate remedies to effective practices that will support our young people.

My parting words are these: school counselors, embrace your creativity every day, in whatever form that may be. Visually, musically, dramatically, or through dance or movement, you deserve to reap the benefits of art. With any art form, you are able to uncover valuable information and help us face what we need to reach our goals and live the life we truly want. Step back and reflect on what you see through your art. After all, when you are in tune with yourself and care for yourself as much as you do your students, your practice with them will be strong and sustainable. Allow yourself to express and be free in your art form. There is no right or wrong, and you have so much to discover about yourself, your practice, and your students. Often, what you are looking for can simply be created and found by no one else but you.

Appendix

Lesson Plans

Copyright material from Arroyo, L.d. (2025) *Integrating Art Therapy Approaches in School Counseling.* Routledge

Lesson Plan 2.1

Lesson Plan Information	
Lesson Plan Title:	Self-Identity Flags
Type of Session/Lesson (Check one):	☐ Individual Counseling ☐ Small Group ☐ Classroom Instruction
Target Audience:	Kindergarten to 12th Grade
Counseling Theory:	Person-Centered, Adlerian (small group and classroom)
Evidence Base:	

☐ Best Practice	☐ Research-Informed
☐ Action Research	☐ Evidence-Based

ASCA Student Standards Targeted:		Student Learning Objectives:
Identify 1–2 student standards relevant for this targeted group and goal:		For each of the selected student standards, write or select 1–2 learning objectives
M&B#	Mindsets & Behaviors Statement	Student Learning Objectives
M2	Sense of acceptance, respect, support, and inclusion for self and others in the school environment	Student(s) will: Learn the value of who they are which includes their values, interests, cultural backgrounds, experiences.
B SS-10	Cultural awareness, sensitivity, and responsiveness	Learn the value of understanding, accepting, and respecting others—even when they are different from who they are.

Copyright material from Arroyo, L.d. (2025) *Integrating Art Therapy Approaches in School Counseling.* Routledge

Materials:
Laptop for school counselor Laptops for students (upper grades) Paper and pencils for sketching Self-Identity Flag worksheet Blank white flags with dowel rods or sheets of rectangle-shaped multimedia paper Fabric markers and paint History of flags from books or web pages to share with students. Examples to include and explain the history and symbols of the Olympic Flag, US Flag, other national and city flags.

Describe How You Will:	
Introduce Lesson Topic/Focus:	Introduce the lesson by letting students know they are going to participate in a self-identity lesson. They will explore more about themselves – their interests, values, backgrounds, and anything else that is meaningful to them.
Communicate the Lesson Objective:	Share with the students that by the end of the lesson, they will have a flag that represents who they are. The goal is to for them to have something that promotes a positive sense of self and to be able to share this with others.
Teach Content:	Explain to students that historically flags represented a group of people by culture, country, or any other affiliation that represented their identity. Discuss commonly seen flags such as the US Flag, or their city flag, Olympic flags and history behind how they were designed. Emphasize the use of flags to demonstrate pride in who they are and how they identify. Today they will start exploring symbols, colors, and other things they can include in their flag, representing their identity. Explain to the students that having a positive self-identity has several benefits. Begin by asking students the questions below. (Modify language for primary grade students.) • How many here have a goal of graduating from kindergarten/middle/high school one day? • How many of you want a career where you can use your interests, talents, knowledge, and skills?

Copyright material from Arroyo, L.d. (2025) *Integrating Art Therapy Approaches in School Counseling*. Routledge

Describe How You Will:	
	• How many of you understand that achieving goals can sometimes be challenging? • How many of you believe that using our strengths (ie. Being a good listener, helping others, being active in sports or in their community, exploring our talents in music, art, dance) will help you get through these challenges? Connect the reasons for positive self-identity to the answers students provided above. Having a positive self-identity has been shown to: • Building self-confidence helps you work through challenges. • Knowing who you are helps you work towards a career that is aligned with who you are, and in turn, could be rewarding and fulfilling. • Knowing who you are helps with self-acceptance. • Accepting and valuing yourself will make you more likely to value others. • Valuing others makes working with others more positive and productive.
Practice Content:	Worksheet: Students can answer the questions that will help them to design their flag. • What does your name mean? What does your name mean to you? • What is your cultural/ethnic background? • What are your favorite colors? • What do you value? (i.e. kindness, fairness, respect) • What are your hobbies, talents, or interests? • What are three things you like about yourself? • What brings you joy? Provide students with laptops, sketch paper, and pencils. Explain that they will explore themes, colors, symbols that represent who they are. Encourage them to use the answers from their worksheet as a reference. They can use their sketch paper to draw out symbols they want to include in their flag. Once they've done their research, they can start sketching out what they'd like their flag to look like. Once they are ready to create their flag, provide the fabric, fabric markers and/or paint, and dowels rods.

Copyright material from Arroyo, L.d. (2025) *Integrating Art Therapy Approaches in School Counseling.* Routledge

Describe How You Will:	
Summarize/ Close:	Have students reflect on their flag and write about how the experience of making their identity flag was for them. Invite students to do a gallery walk of all of the flags created in the class. Ask students to share their experiences and invite any questions or comments or observations about the work (i.e. I noticed a lot of people used this symbol, color, word, etc). Ask them what it was like sharing, whether verbally or visually through their flag, who they are with others. Does it feel comfortable? Or a little scary? Welcome a range of emotions and reactions. Facilitate a discussion with the students on why it is important to know ourselves and others. Would it lead to more understancing and acceptance of each other? How would it affect our classrooms? Our school? Summarize the lesson by sharing your observations of the flags, the uniqueness of each one. Also acknowledge their participation, in particular viewing others' flags, and demonstrating genuine curiosity about their classmates and who they are as represented in the flags.

Data Collection Plan	
Participation Data Plan:	
Anticipated number of students:	1 – Individual School Counseling 3–6 Small Group 15+ Classroom Instruction
Planned length of lesson(s):	30–45 minutes

ASCA Student Standards Data Plan:

Pre-/Post-Assessment Items are:
1 I belong at school, and I make sure everyone else feels welcome too.
2 I feel comfortable at school and make sure that others feel comfortable too.
3 I understand that everyone has their own unique culture and background.
4 I believe it is important to learn about the cultures and backgrounds of others that are different than my own.

Outcome Data Plan:

Achievement: Students' academic achievement as measured through GPA, number of D's and F's, test scores, or other metric that measures academic progress will be compared at the beginning and at the end of the intervention.

Copyright material from Arroyo, L.d. (2025) *Integrating Art Therapy Approaches in School Counseling.* Routledge

Follow-Up Plans
Students who miss this lesson can make it up during a make-up session planned and facilitated by the school counselor. For students who did not demonstrate mastery on the pre-/post-assessment of student standards (M&B)/student learning objectives, the school counselor, in collaboration with other team members such as members of the behavioral health team, the student's teacher(s), and parent, will determine if a different or more intensive intervention is needed.

Self-Identity Flag

Answer the questions below to help you design your flag.

- What does your name mean? What does your name mean to you?

- What is your cultural/ ethnic background?

- What are your favorite colors?

- What do you value? (i.e. kindness, fairness, respect)

- What are your hobbies, talents, or interests?

- What are 3 things you like about yourself?

- What makes you happy?

Copyright material from Arroyo, L.d. (2025) *Integrating Art Therapy Approaches in School Counseling.* Routledge

Now look up some pictures, symbols, and images that represent the information above.

Sketch out ideas for your flag.

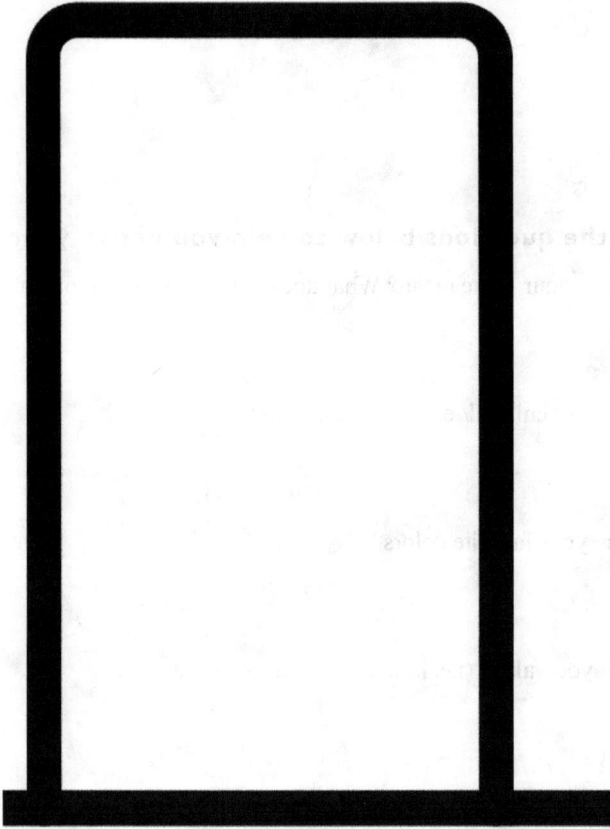

Copyright material from Arroyo, L.d. (2025) *Integrating Art Therapy Approaches in School Counseling*. Routledge

Lesson Plan 2.2

Lesson Plan Information	
Lesson Plan Title:	Animal for a Day
Type of Session/Lesson (Check one):	☐ Individual Counseling ☐ Small Group ☐ Classroom Instruction
Target Audience:	Kindergarten to 12th Grade
Counseling Theory:	Adlerian Theory
Evidence Base:	
☐ Best Practice ☐ Action Research	☐ Research-Informed ☐ Evidence-Based

ASCA Student Standards Targeted:		Student Learning Objectives:
Identify 1–2 student standards relevant for this targeted group and goal:		For each of the selected student standards, write or select 1–2 learning objectives
M&B#	Mindsets & Behaviors Statement	Student Learning Objectives
M2.	Sense of acceptance, respect, support, and inclusion for self and others in the school environment	Student(s) will: Show respect for themselves as they learn more about what makes them unique. Learn how to get along with others even when they may have different interests, experiences, backgrounds, and opinions.

Copyright material from Arroyo, L.d. (2025) *Integrating Art Therapy Approaches in School Counseling.* Routledge

Materials:
Part I: air dry clay, plastic utensils or other tools to help shape the clay, baby wipes, and cleaning wipes for quick clean-up, pictures of animals for reference; plastic tray, placemat, or wax paper for each student to keep table clean and clay within boundaries Part II: acrylic paint and brushes, cups/glass jars of water, and plastic plates or lids to use as paint palettes, glue

Describe How You Will:	
Introduce Lesson Topic/ Focus:	Inform students that they will learn more about themselves and others, and how that affects a shared space and a safe community.
Communicate the Lesson Objective:	Explain to students that they will learn more about themselves as they identify their strengths and challenges, those of others, and how that knowledge can help everyone feel comfortable in a shared space such as school.
Teach Content:	Explain to the students that they will be participating in an art activity will span over two sessions or lessons. The goal is for them recognize how they can contribute to a positive school environment by knowing more about themselves and each other. Ask students why it is important for everyone to feel comfortable at school. Offer examples such as feeling comfortable, will help students to be motivated to come to school, resulting in their ability to learn.
Practice Content:	Part I: Provide students with a handful of air-dry clay. Let them play with the clay - stretch, press, pinch, and pound gently - to see how it responds. They can also use plastic utensils or other safe tools to create designs, texture, etc. Demonstrate students how students can attach pieces of clay together by smoothing the clay pieces onto each other with a plastic utensil, creating a slip (combination of water and clay) to adhere pieces together. Once they have gotten comfortable working with the clay, ask students if they could be an animal for one day, what animal would that be? Direct them to create that animal with clay. Students can refer to pictures of animals for inspiration.

Copyright material from Arroyo, L.d. (2025) *Integrating Art Therapy Approaches in School Counseling.* Routledge

Describe How You Will:	
	Inform students that the clay is an air dry clay, so it will be allowed to dry until the next session, when they will paint their animals. If any students are finished early, they may be given more clay to make items that will help their animals feel safe and taken care of (i.e. carrots if the animal is a bunny, a blanket for a cat to lay on) Part II: When the clay animals are completely dry, students can use fine sandpaper to gently smooth out cracks and rough spots on their animals. If any parts broke apart, they can use glue to piece their animal back together. Students can then paint their animals. When students are done painting, ask students to share what animal they chose and why. Ask them what the strengths of their animals are (i.e. a bunny has large ears that may help them hear well, a giraffe has a long neck and can reach for things up high) as well as any challenges they may have (i.e. a turtle is not very fast, a deer becomes startled easily).
Summarize/ Close:	Part I Ask students what was it like to work with clay. Were they excited, or did they feel frustrated? If they had difficulty with the clay, did they problem-solve on their own? Or ask others for for assistance? Help students recognize how being with others while working on something fun or challenging can be helpful. They can ask for help, ask each other for help, ask the counselor for help. How can this be translated to other places where they are with others, such as the classroom? Part II Direct students to paint their animals now that they are dry. Students can place them in the center of the table. Ask the group what needs to be in the space for all animals to feel safe and cared for. This can lead to a discussion on what makes them feel safe and taken care of at school. Discuss how the group members have empathy for other animals who may have challenges (i.e. being slow, shy, startled easily, quick to react, etc.) and how that can translate to having empathy for themselves, and for others in their class and the school community. Students can be asked how this relates to students taking the lead in creating a positive school environment.

Copyright material from Arroyo, L.d. (2025) *Integrating Art Therapy Approaches in School Counseling*. Routledge

Data Collection Plan	
Participation Data Plan:	
Anticipated number of students:	1 – Individual School Counseling 3–6 Small Group 15+ Classroom Instruction
Planned length of lesson(s):	30–45 minutes
ASCA Student Standards Data Plan:	
Pre-/Post-Assessment Items are: 1 I belong at school and I make sure everyone else feels welcome too. 2 I feel comfortable at school and make sure that others feel comfortable too.	
Outcome Data Plan:	
Achievement: Students' academic achievement as measured through GPA, number of D's and F's, test scores, or other metric that measures academic progress will be compared at the beginning and at the end of the intervention.	
Follow-Up Plans	
Students who miss this lesson can make it up during a make-up session planned and facilitated by the school counselor. For students who did not demonstrate mastery on the pre-/post-assessment of student standards (M&B)/student learning objectives, the school counselor, in collaboration with other team members such as members of the behavioral health team, the student's teacher(s), and parent, will determine if a different or more intensive intervention is needed.	

Copyright material from Arroyo, L.d. (2025) *Integrating Art Therapy Approaches in School Counseling.* Routledge

Lesson Plan 3.1

Lesson Plan Information	
Lesson Plan Title:	Graduation Day
Type of Session/Lesson (Check one):	☐ Individual Counseling ☐ Small Group ☐ Classroom Instruction
Target Audience:	6th to 12th Grade Students
Counseling Theory:	Person-Centered Theory
Evidence Base:	

☐ Best Practice ☐ Action Research	☐ Research-Informed ☐ Evidence-Based

ASCA Student Standards Targeted:		Student Learning Objectives:
Identify 1–2 student standards relevant for this targeted group and goal:		For each of the selected student standards, write or select 1–2 learning objectives
M&B#	Mindsets & Behaviors Statement	Student Learning Objectives
M 4. B-LS 4.	Self-confidence in ability to succeed Self-motivation and self-direction for learning	Student(s) will: Identify an academic goal and believe they can achieve it. Identify resources and action steps to help them reach their goal.

Copyright material from Arroyo, L.d. (2025) *Integrating Art Therapy Approaches in School Counseling*. Routledge

Materials:
Mixed media paper 12″ × 18″ 15+ Silhouette of student in cap and gown on cardstock Graphite pencils Erasers Colored pencils Markers Optional: Emoji or motivational quote stickers or other decorative stickers

Describe How You Will:	
Introduce Lesson Topic/ Focus:	Inform students that they will identify an academic goal for the school year and identify ways to achieve it.
Communicate the Lesson Objective:	Explain to students that the goal of the lesson is to help them understand that they play a large role in their success. By the end of the lesson, they will be able to identify a goal, create an art piece to help them believe they can achieve their goal, and identify resources to get them to their goal.
Teach Content:	Start the lesson by sharing data related to being successful academically, such as attendance to school, coming to school on time, turning in all of their homework, and effective study habits. Inform students that having this information is beneficial to help them make informed decisions during the school year, and they can determine how they want their school year to go. From there they can take the action steps needed to ultimately reach their goals. Ask students if they would like to see themselves graduating that year (or number of years until graduation) and going on to their college, career, or other pathway of choice such as military or apprenticeship. If there is a collective yes, acknowledge this for the class and let them know that by identifying this as a goal, and the steps to get there, will increase their likelihood of this happening in their future.

Copyright material from Arroyo, L.d. (2025) *Integrating Art Therapy Approaches in School Counseling.* Routledge

Describe How You Will:	
Practice Content:	Instruct students to trace a silhouette of a student in a cap and gown onto their paper. Students will then draw what they would look like on Graduation Day. They will envision what that day would look like - who would be there, what they would be feeling and thinking, and any other factors they felt would be important to include in their Graduation Day drawings. They can add where they will go next, as well as any evidence such as report card grades that help them see that they are on their way to reach their goal. Students will discuss and reflect on the art-making process. This can be done by having students share their art with a partner or through a gallery walk (described in Chapter 5). Ask for volunteers to share with the class what they can start doing today to get them to their goal (i.e. checking their current grades, studying earlier for exams, asking for help).
Summarize/ Close:	Ask for volunteers to share what their experience was like to create their graduation day drawings and what it was like to see their classmates' drawings. Explain to students that their art can serve as a visual reminder and inspiration to achieve their goals. Recommend that they display their drawings in a place where they can see it and serve as motivation throughout the year.

Data Collection Plan	
Participation Data Plan:	
Anticipated number of students:	1 – Individual School Counseling 3–6 Small Group 15+ Classroom Instruction
Planned length of lesson(s):	30–45 minutes
ASCA Student Standards Data Plan:	

Pre-/Post-Assessment items are:
1 I can state at least one academic goal for this school year.
2 I can identify two actions steps I can start today to reach my goals for the future.
3 I know how to keep myself motivated to obtain my goals.
4 I believe my actions play a part in being successful in school.

Copyright material from Arroyo, L.d. (2025) *Integrating Art Therapy Approaches in School Counseling*. Routledge

Outcome Data Plan:
Achievement: Students' academic achievement as measured through GPA, number of D's and F's, test scores, or other metric that measures academic progress will be compared at the beginning and at the end of the intervention.
Follow-Up Plans
Students who miss this lesson can make it up during a make-up session planned and facilitated by the school counselor. For students who did not demonstrate mastery on the pre-/post-assessment of student standards (M&B)/student learning objectives, the school counselor, in collaboration with other team members such as members of the behavioral health team, the student's teacher(s), and parent, will determine if a different or more intensive intervention is needed.

Copyright material from Arroyo, L.d. (2025) *Integrating Art Therapy Approaches in School Counseling.* Routledge

Lesson Plan 3.2

Lesson Plan Information	
Lesson Plan Title:	Art for Inspiration
Type of Session/Lesson (Check one):	☐ Individual Counseling ☐ Small Group ☐ Classroom Instruction
Target Audience:	3rd to 12th Grade
Counseling Theory:	Cognitive Behavioral Theory
Evidence base:	
☐ Best Practice ☐ Action Research	☐ Research-Informed ☐ Evidence-Based

ASCA Student Standards Targeted:		Student Learning Objectives:
Identify 1–2 student standards relevant for this targeted group and goal:		For each of the selected student standards, write or select 1–2 learning objectives
M&B#	Mindsets & Behaviors Statement	Student Learning Objectives
B-SMS 5. B-SMS 6.	Perseverance to achieve long- and short-term goals Ability to identify and overcome barriers	Student(s) will: Create inspirational reminders that will inspire them reach their goals. Identify strategies to use when they are experiencing difficulties in obtaining their goals.

Copyright material from Arroyo, L.d. (2025) *Integrating Art Therapy Approaches in School Counseling.* Routledge

Materials:	
Stickers or printouts of inspirational quotes and phrases, oil pastels, markers, colored pencils, 4 1/2" × 6" or 9" × 12" mixed media paper	

Describe How You Will:	
Introduce Lesson Topic/ Focus:	Inform students that the lesson today is a follow up to previous lessons about goal setting (for example, short-term goals related to improving grades and attendance, or long-term goals such as college admission, starting their dream career)
Communicate the Lesson Objective:	Explain that the objective for the lesson is to understand that many times reaching goals can be difficult, but they can get through challenges positively through inspiration, and identifying resources and action steps to get there.
Teach Content:	Lead a discussion on what can make reaching goals difficult. For example, when discussing academics, challenges include being nervous before tests, not understanding homework, not getting enough sleep, having a fight with a friend, etc. Acknowledge that challenges can be hard, but when they are inspired and reminded of their goal, they can feel more motivated rather than giving up. Feeling inspired will also help identify action steps to reach goals. For example, asking for help when needed, or staying off social media before bedtime, etc. Ask students what goals they have for the school year or in the future (ex. Dream Career, to do well in math, go to high school or college of choice, etc.) Each student can write it down or share out loud if in a small group or individual counseling session. Ask students to discuss if anything makes it hard for themselves or anyone to achieve their goals (math problems are hard, feeling sad, etc.). Lead a discussion on what encourages them. What helps them to feel inspired and encouraged to keep doing their best? Discuss positive ways to work through challenges, such as positive self-talk, positive words, phrases, and talking to friends or trusted adults about goals.

Copyright material from Arroyo, L.d. (2025) *Integrating Art Therapy Approaches in School Counseling.* Routledge

Describe How You Will:	
	Ask students if they ever felt motivated or inspired before, and if they would like to share their stories. Acknowledge how the students persevered through difficult times and challenges by being motivated and inspired. Explain to students that visual inspiration can remind them of their goals and how to get through challenges. They will each have the opportunity to create their art for inspiration.
Practice Content:	Students should each have a sheet of mixed media paper and sets of oil pastels, markers, and colored pencils. Students will pick one sticker with a quote or phrase that could help them during challenging times and place it anywhere on their drawing paper. They will draw around their quotes and fill the space around their stickers. They can draw lines, forms, colors, shapes, write additional words, etc.
Summarize/ Close:	The school counselor can ask each student to share their drawing (small group or individual counseling) or share with a partner in a classroom. Students will be encouraged to ask each other questions such as, why did you pick that quote? How did you choose the colors, images, lines, etc., for your drawing? Which part of your drawing stands out to you? How does it feel to look at your drawing? Close the lesson/session with a discussion of how they can use their drawings to stay inspired should any challenges come up along the way. They can hang it somewhere they will see it daily, or take a picture of it to save to their phone, etc. From there, they can ask themselves if their daily practices align with their goals (i.e. are they completing all assignments, are they getting enough sleep, are they asking for help).

Copyright material from Arroyo, L.d. (2025) *Integrating Art Therapy Approaches in School Counseling*. Routledge

Data Collection Plan	
Participation Data Plan:	
Anticipated number of students:	1 – Individual School Counseling 3–6 Small Group 15+ Classroom Instruction
Planned length of lesson(s):	30–45 minutes
ASCA Student Standards Data Plan:	

Pre-/Post-Assessment items are:
1 I can name two ways to get help when I am having a hard time reaching my goals.
2 I know how to deal with stressful situations in a way that is helpful and positive.
3 I can define inspiration.
4 I know how to keep myself inspired to reach my goals through difficult times.

Outcome Data Plan:

Achievement: Students' academic achievement as measured through GPA, number of D's and F's, test scores, or other metric that measures academic progress will be compared at the beginning and at the end of the intervention.

Follow-Up Plans

Students who miss this lesson can make it up during a make-up session planned and facilitated by the school counselor.

For students who did not demonstrate mastery on the pre-/post-assessment of student standards (M&B)/student learning objectives, the school counselor, in collaboration with other team members such as members of the behavioral health team, the student's teacher(s), and parent, will determine if a different or more intensive intervention is needed.

Copyright material from Arroyo, L.d. (2025) *Integrating Art Therapy Approaches in School Counseling.* Routledge

Lesson Plan 3.3

Lesson Plan Information	
Lesson Plan Title:	Art Card
Type of Session/Lesson (Check one):	☐ Individual Counseling ☐ Small Group ☐ Classroom Instruction
Target Audience:	Kindergarten to 12th Grade
Counseling Theory:	Adlerian
Evidence Base:	

☐ Best Practice ☐ Action Research	☐ Research-Informed ☐ Evidence-Based

ASCA Student Standards Targeted:		Student Learning Objectives:
Identify 1–2 student standards relevant for this targeted group and goal:		For each of the selected student standards, write or select 1–2 learning objectives
M&B#	Mindsets & Behaviors Statement	Student Learning Objectives
M.2	Sense of acceptance, respect, support, and inclusion for self and others in the school environment	Students will create a visual reminder of the value they hold for themselves. Students will create a visual reminder for their peers representing the value they hold for them and to support their growth after the last session.

Copyright material from Arroyo, L.d. (2025) *Integrating Art Therapy Approaches in School Counseling.* Routledge

Materials:	
Mixed media paper, markers, colored pencils, stickers, pre-cut images, and other items.	

Describe How You Will:	
Introduce Lesson Topic/Focus:	Inform students today's session will summarize what they've learned during their time in small group.
Communicate the Lesson Objective:	Explain to the group that they will have a visual reminder of the important lessons they learned about themselves and others, to serve as inspiration and motivation to continue using what they've learned after today.
Teach Content:	Explain to students that the purpose of their time spent in together over the past several weeks was to learn skills that can help them be successful in school and life. This included learning more about themselves and others, and how that helps to relate well with each other, and have a sense of belonging at school. Ask each student to share what were some of the important lessons they've learned in the group. Explain that they will create a visual reminder of these lessons learned in the art activity today.
Practice Content:	Instruct students to fold their papers in half to make a card. Ask them to write their name on the front of their card the in any way they want. Once everyone has finished their name drawings, ask them to share what they created, as well as what they enjoyed about being in the small group. Students will then pass their cards to the person next to them, who will create something inside their fellow group member's card. It could be a symbol, design, message, etc., something for the card owner to remember them by. The cards will be passed around until it comes back to the original owner. Each group member should have drawn something in each group member's card.

Copyright material from Arroyo, L.d. (2025) *Integrating Art Therapy Approaches in School Counseling*. Routledge

Describe How You Will:	
Summarize/Close:	Ask students to share what it was like to draw in each other's cards, and how they felt once they received their card back. Students can share what they see inside their cards. Encourage students to continue taking care of themselves and respecting others, in other spaces in and outside of school. If they need motivation and inspiration, they can look at their art cards.

Data Collection Plan	
Participation Data Plan:	
Anticipated number of students:	1 – Individual School Counseling 3–6 Small Group 15+ Classroom Instruction
Planned length of lesson(s):	30–45 minutes
ASCA Student Standards Data Plan:	
Pre-/Post-Assessment Items are: 1 I belong at school, and I make sure everyone else feels welcome too. 2 I feel comfortable at school and make sure that others feel comfortable too.	
Outcome Data Plan:	
Achievement: Students' academic achievement as measured through GPA, number of D's and F's, test scores, or other metric that measures academic progress will be compared at the beginning and at the end of the intervention.	
Follow-Up Plans	
Students who miss this lesson can make it up during a make-up session planned and facilitated by the school counselor. For students who did not demonstrate mastery on the pre-/post-assessment of student standards (M&B)/student learning objectives, the school counselor, in collaboration with other team members such as members of the behavioral health team, the student's teacher(s), and parent, will determine if a different or more intensive intervention is needed.	

Copyright material from Arroyo, L.d. (2025) *Integrating Art Therapy Approaches in School Counseling*. Routledge

Lesson Plan 4.1

Lesson Plan Information	
Lesson Plan Title:	Continuous Line Drawing with Oil Pastels
Type of Session/Lesson (Check one):	☐ Individual Counseling ☐ Small Group ☐ Classroom Instruction
Target Audience:	Kindergarten to 12th Grade
Counseling Theory:	Person-Centered
Evidence Base:	
☐ Best Practice ☐ Action Research	☐ Research-Informed ☐ Evidence-Based

ASCA Student Standards Targeted:		Student Learning Objectives:
Identify 1–2 student standards relevant for this targeted group and goal:		For each of the selected student standards, write or select 1–2 learning objectives
M&B#	Mindsets and Behaviors Statement	Student Learning Objectives
B-SMS 7	Effective coping skills	Student(s) will: Develop and apply strategies to manage stressful situations in a positive way.

Copyright material from Arroyo, L.d. (2025) *Integrating Art Therapy Approaches in School Counseling.* Routledge

Materials:	
9" × 12" Mixed media paper Set of oil pastels for each student Black marker for each student Baby wipes Calming music – classical, smooth jazz, other instrumental music, or nature sounds	

Describe How You Will:	

Introduce
  Lesson Topic/
  Focus:
	Inform students that they will participate in an art activity to help them when feeling worried, nervous, stressed, or anxious.

Communicate
  the Lesson
  Objective:
	Inform students that the lesson's goal is for them to learn a positive way to cope when feeling these emotions.

Teach Content:	Explain to students that feeling stressed or anxious can feel overwhelming. Lead a discussion with students on what types of situations can cause stress and how people cope with stress. Address the results when people negatively deal with stress, for example, keeping to themselves, escaping through video games or social media. Address results of positively dealing with stress, such as asking for help, talking to a friend, exercising, listening to music. Share with them that according to studies, the simple activities, such as creating art, no matter how simple the materials, can help a person calm down. Demonstrate for students how they will do a continuous line drawing on their paper, moving the black marker on the paper without lifting for one minute. Once the line drawing is complete, demonstrate the different ways of using oil pastels – use at the point and create marks, turn it on its side to make a different type of mark. Also demonstrate the blending of two or more colors together, smear with fingers, or layering oil pastel colors one on top of the other. Inform students that each person's art will look different, and that there is no right or wrong way their drawing should look. Remind that the baby wipes are there for a quick cleanup of their hands once they are done with their art.

Copyright material from Arroyo, L.d. (2025) *Integrating Art Therapy Approaches in School Counseling.* Routledge

Describe How You Will:	
Practice Content:	Students will create their continuous line drawing for one minute, then continue adding to their drawings with oil pastels for 10–15 minutes while music plays softly in the background.
Summarize/ Close:	Facilitate a discussion and reflection on the art-making process among the students. This can be done by having students share their art with a partner or through a gallery walk (described in Chapter 5). Encourage students to ask one another questions, such as, what was it like to work on this type of drawing? What did you notice as you started working with the oil pastels? Is there anything that stands out to you in your drawing? Do you see common themes in everyone's drawings such as colors, and shapes? Is each art piece unique? How so? How did you feel while working on your drawing? Explain to students that participation in a simple art activity can help a person calm down when feeling stressed or worried. Share how they can create art outside of their session to help them calm down. Acknowledge for students that there may be times that they are not able to draw (i.e. in the middle of class, lunch, recess, or when they don't have access to materials). Lead a discussion on what else they can do to calm down in a positive and effective way when they are stressed (talk to a friend or trusted adult, take deep breaths, move around, or stretch).

Data Collection Plan	
Participation Data Plan:	
Anticipated number of students:	1 – Individual school counseling 3–6 Small group 15+ Classroom instruction
Planned length of lesson(s):	30–45 minutes
ASCA Student Standards Data Plan:	

Pre-/Post-Assessment items are:
1 I know how to calm down and feel better when I'm upset or having a tough time.
2 I know how to deal with stressful situations in a way that is helpful and positive.

Copyright material from Arroyo, L.d. (2025) *Integrating Art Therapy Approaches in School Counseling.* Routledge

Outcome Data Plan:

Achievement: Students' academic achievement as measured through GPA, number of D's and F's, test scores, or other metric that measures academic progress will be compared at the beginning and at the end of the intervention.

Follow-Up Plans

Students who miss this lesson can make it up during a make-up session planned and facilitated by the school counselor.

For students who did not demonstrate mastery on the pre-/post-assessment of student standards (M&B)/student learning objectives, the school counselor, in collaboration with other team members such as members of the behavioral health team, the student's teacher(s), and parent, will determine if a different or more intensive intervention is needed.

Copyright material from Arroyo, L.d. (2025) *Integrating Art Therapy Approaches in School Counseling.* Routledge

Lesson Plan 4.2

Lesson Plan Information	
Lesson Plan Title:	Emoji Drawings
Type of Session/Lesson (Check one):	☐ Individual Counseling ☐ Small Group ☐ Classroom Instruction
Target Audience:	Kindergarten to 12th Grade Students
Counseling Theory:	Cognitive Behavioral Theory
Evidence Base:	
☐ Best Practice ☐ Action Research	☐ Research Informed ☐ Evidence Based

ASCA Student Standards Targeted:		Student Learning Objectives:
Identify 1–2 student standards relevant for this targeted group and goal:		For each of the selected student standards, write or select 1–2 learning objectives
M&B#	Mindsets & Behaviors Statement	Student Learning Objectives
B-SMS 1 B-SMS 2	B-SMS 1. Responsibility for self and actions Self-discipline and self-control	Student(s) will: Understand that they can experience a range of emotions. Understand how their feelings are based on their thoughts of different situations. Understand how they feel can affect how they act.

Copyright material from Arroyo, L.d. (2025) *Integrating Art Therapy Approaches in School Counseling.* Routledge

Materials:
Emoji Stickers or printouts of different emoji expressions, 9" × 12" multimedia paper, colored pencils, markers, and Emoji Lesson Scenarios Worksheet

Describe How You Will:	
Introduce Lesson Topic/Focus:	Inform students that they will be discussing different emotions and how they can affect how they act. They will also understand the thoughts behind the emotions they feel based on different scenarios.
Communicate the Lesson Objective:	Explain to students that understanding a range of our emotions helps us to better understand ourselves and, as a result, be able to manage emotions. This can help them develop healthy relationships and make positive decisions.
Teach Content:	Ask students if they ever felt so strongly that they ended up doing something they felt sorry about later (i.e. talking back to a parent or teacher, getting into a fight with a friend). Students can raise their hands and if comfortable, share about that time. Inform students that feeling strongly doesn't always lead to behavior that they will regret later. Ask students to volunteer what their typical reaction they have when they hear good news (students may share that they feel happy, which can lead them to jump up and down in excitement). Explain to students that they will better understand how they feel in different situations can impact how they react. They will also recognize a step that comes before that, which is what they think, or their thoughts about certain situations, can lead them to how they feel. They can think of a cycle going from Thought to Feeling to Action, and back to the Thought where the cycle starts again.

Copyright material from Arroyo, L.d. (2025) *Integrating Art Therapy Approaches in School Counseling*. Routledge

Describe How You Will:	
Practice Content:	Instruct students to number their papers from 1-5. Let them know that each number represents a scenario that will be read to them. Read a scenario (Choose up to 5 sample scenarios or create ones based on common events at school.). Instruct students to pick one to two emoji stickers in response to each scenario and place them next to the number of the scenario. After they place their stickers on their paper, ask students to share why they picked the emoji(s) sticker for the particular scenario. Ask them to discuss their initial thoughts about the scenario, and if this relates to the emoji they picked. Then ask them what action steps they would take in response to each scenario. Do this after each scenario until they are done. After each scenario is read, lead a discussion on how thoughts affected the emoji that the students picked for each one. Discuss how sometimes irrational thoughts, or thoughts not based on facts, can lead to emotions that will lead them to act in a way that they may regret later. For each scenario, share with students a different way of thinking about a scenario. For example, if they weren't invited to a party, instead of thinking, "I'm not popular, nobody likes me." Another thought could be, "I may not have been invited, but that doesn't mean I'm not likable." Then discuss the ability to examine thoughts more closely, as they know that this step can affect how they feel and act. Recommend to students that when they feel overwhelmed, they can pause, take a breath, and think first.
Summarize/Close:	To close out the session, inform students that they will express how they feel right now. They will choose emoji stickers (there can be more than one but limit to 5) based on current emotions. They can then place the stickers anywhere on their paper and draw around their emoji stickers to emphasize their emotions. Review for students that emotions can be helpful, allowing for deeper knowledge of themselves, and helping to make positive choices that will help in and out of school.

Copyright material from Arroyo, L.d. (2025) *Integrating Art Therapy Approaches in School Counseling.* Routledge

Data Collection Plan	
Participation Data Plan:	
Anticipated number of students:	1 – Individual School Counseling 3–6 Small Group 15+ Classroom Instruction
Planned length of lesson(s):	30–45 minutes
ASCA Student Standards Data Plan:	
Pre-/Post-Assessment items are: 1 I can have more than one emotion at a time. 2 Emotions can give us valuable information about ourselves. 3 Thoughts affect how I feel. 4 How I feel can affect how I act.	
Outcome Data Plan:	
Achievement: Students' academic achievement as measured through GPA, number of D's and F's, test scores, or other metric that measures academic progress will be compared at the beginning and at the end of the intervention.	
Follow-Up Plans	
Students who miss this lesson can make it up during a make-up session planned and facilitated by the school counselor. For students who did not demonstrate mastery of the pre-/post-assessment of student standards (M&B)/student learning objectives, the school counselor, in collaboration with other team members such as members of the behavioral health team, the student's teacher(s), and parent, will determine if a different or more intensive intervention is needed.	

Copyright material from Arroyo, L.d. (2025) *Integrating Art Therapy Approaches in School Counseling.* Routledge

Emoji Lesson Scenarios

Kindergarten to Second Grades:

"How would you feel if another classmate took turns on the slide with you at recess?"

"How would you feel if you couldn't find your favorite stuffed animal or toy?"

"How would you feel if you had a stomach ache?"

"How would you feel if your classmates weren't sharing?"

"How would you feel if you didn't understand something the teacher said?"

"How would you feel if no one sat with you at lunch or asked you to play at recess?"

Third to Eight Grades:

"How would you feel if you got the winning point in a game at recess or gym?"

"How would you feel if, every time your parent or guardian came up to school, the students made fun of them because of the way they looked or talked?"

"How would you feel if someone helped you solve a problem?"

"How would you feel if someone you admire called you a name you didn't like?"

"How would you feel if someone told you they were sorry after they tripped you?"

"How would you feel if you didn't understand the class assignment?"

"How would you feel if your class won a pizza party?"

Seventh to Twelfth Grades:

"How would you feel if someone asked your advice about a problem?"

Copyright material from Arroyo, L.d. (2025) *Integrating Art Therapy Approaches in School Counseling.* Routledge

"How would you feel if you didn't get invited to a party that the rest of your friends were invited to?"

"How would you feel if you were asked to give a presentation in the auditorium?"

"How would you feel if you didn't understand the homework assignment?"

"How would you feel if you received a grade of C or below on your test after studying so hard?"

"How would you feel if you did not get a text back from your friend who normally responds right away?"

"How would you feel if you were sitting or lying down comfortably listening to your favorite music?"

Copyright material from Arroyo, L.d. (2025) *Integrating Art Therapy Approaches in School Counseling.* Routledge

Index

Note: **Bold** page numbers refer to tables and *italic* page numbers refer to figures.

For Product Safety Concerns and Information please contact our EU
representative GPSR@taylorandfrancis.com
Taylor & Francis Verlag GmbH, Kaufingerstraße 24, 80331 München, Germany

www.ingramcontent.com/pod-product-compliance
Lightning Source LLC
Chambersburg PA
CBHW070339270326
41926CB00017B/3921

* 9 7 8 1 0 3 2 5 5 4 9 1 4 *